Perplexed Prophets

PERPLEXED PROPHETS

SIX NINETEENTH-CENTURY

BRITISH AUTHORS

By Gaylord C. LeRoy

GREENWOOD PRESS, PUBLISHERS
WESTPORT, CONNECTICUT

Copyright 1953 by Temple University

Originally published in 1953
by University of Pennsylvania Press for
Temple University Publications, Philadelphia

Reprinted with the permission
of University of Pennsylvania Press

First Greenwood Reprinting 1971

Library of Congress Catalogue Card Number 78-147220

SBN 8371-5985-7

Printed in the United States of America

ACKNOWLEDGMENTS

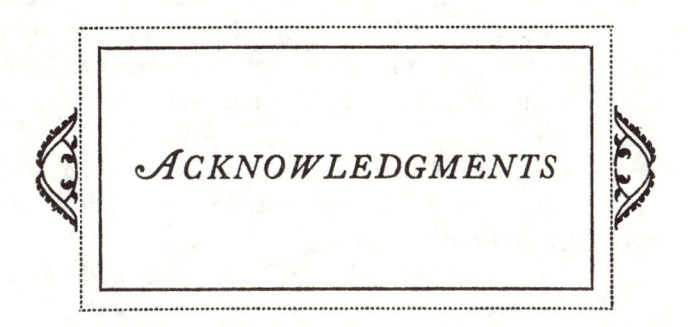

PART OF THE MATERIAL IN THE CHAPTER ON RUSKIN HAS appeared in different form in *The Modern Language Quarterly* and *The South Atlantic Quarterly,* and an earlier version of a small portion of the chapter on Arnold was published in *College English.* I wish to thank the editors of these three journals for giving me permission to use this material here.

I want to acknowledge my sense of indebtedness to two professors, now dead, under whom I studied the literature of the Victorian period as an undergraduate and a graduate student: Professor Charles H. A. Wager of Oberlin College and Professor Irving Babbitt of Harvard University. Neither would subscribe entirely to the interpretation of the Victorians offered in this book, but my sense of owing a debt to these two teachers, for whom the study of literature was not merely delight but the highroad to an understanding of the nature of man, is none the less for that.

I want to express my gratitude to Temple University for a reduction in teaching load which enabled me to devote time to the writing of this book, and, more important, for providing the kind of cultural climate in which a study of this sort can be congenially pursued.

Special thanks are due to Professors Barrows Dunham and David H. Webster of the Temple University faculty: to Professor Dunham for urging me to carry these studies through to completion and for helping in invaluable ways to clarify my thinking about the Victorian age; to Professor Webster for his careful and pertinacious comments on an earlier draft of the manuscript.

The greatest debt of all I owe to my wife, without whose confidence, encouragement, and assistance the book could not have been written.

GAYLORD C. LeRoy

Temple University
January 1953

Contents

One   INTRODUCTION   1

Two   THOMAS CARLYLE   13

Three   MATTHEW ARNOLD   40

Four   JOHN RUSKIN   86

Five   JAMES THOMSON   104

Six   DANTE GABRIEL ROSSETTI   121

Seven   OSCAR WILDE   148

Eight   CONCLUSION   168

NOTES   181

INDEX   201

One

INTRODUCTION

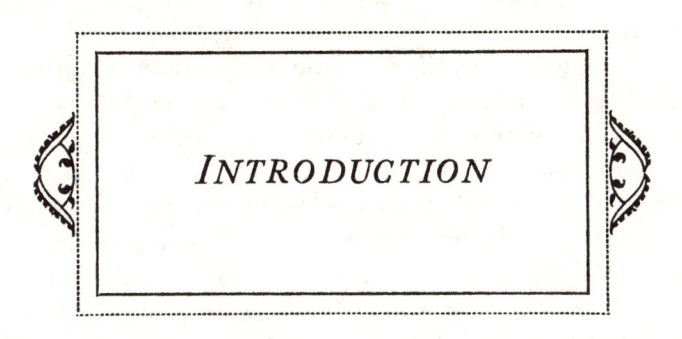

THE AUTHORS I AM DEALING WITH DIFFER FROM ONE ANOTHER considerably. Carlyle was a critic, historian, and philosopher; Arnold a poet and a literary and social critic; Ruskin an art critic and social critic. Thomson is remembered chiefly as poet-pessimist; Rossetti as poet, painter, and initiator of estheticism; Wilde as wit, revolutionary, and esthete. Yet these authors have much in common: the unity of place—England, or rather London; and of time—the last two-thirds, approximately, of the nineteenth century. They have a further unity in that the significant features of the work of each grew out of the way he adjusted himself to a new society, and in the fact that this society, while it changed in important ways from the time of Carlyle to that of Wilde, yet in its main configurations was on the whole the same for all of them.

My aim has been, not to attempt a systematic survey of the work of these poets and critics, but to find out how the significant attitudes shaping the work of each author grew out of the adjustment he achieved between his own personal nature and the new society with which he necessarily established a relationship. I have confined myself, in other words, to an attempt to disclose the source of the distinctive point of view and achievement of each author by making clear the central pattern of his response to the problems of his time.

In the attempt to discover the goals, conflicts, and fears which helped to shape the main outlines of each author's philosophy I have made what use I could of two approaches which together constitute, it seems obvious, the great contributions to the understanding of man made in recent times: study of the inner dynamics of personality, and study of the forms of relatedness between the individual and his society. No student of biography can now dispense with consideration of the unconscious influences of which Freud was the first to speak. Yet to make proper use of such knowledge is difficult. Those who approach an author as a psychiatrist studies a patient and attempt simply to discover the neurotic trends that shaped his personality and work, are almost as likely to misrepresent the situation as to clarify it. We cannot know as much about any author we study as the psychiatrist feels it necessary to know before he attempts to diagnose a patient. When one considers the time and patience required for analysis of a living person, the variety of methods used—dream analysis, free association, searching into forgotten memories—one feels that a student must be rash to attempt a similar investigation of an author who can be studied only through the written word, especially if the written word was set down in a reticent age. Such a study may easily turn out to be little more than guesswork. Who can now know, for example, what infantile experiences were responsible for James Thomson's sense of guilt?

More important, this kind of study often suffers from the same one-sidedness that we see in the work of those psychiatrists who believe that the neurotic trends of childhood provide a sufficient key to adult personality. If the personality is shaped in part by infantile experience, it is also shaped by the society to which the adult relates himself—its hospitality

INTRODUCTION

and hostility, its particular modes of generating security and insecurity. The adult's social relationships serve to perpetuate, to intensify, or to modify and diminish neurotic trends which have their origin in childhood. The writer who attempts a psychological study, however, often loses sight of the fact that the author with whom he is concerned was an adult dealing with the problems of a real environment and treats him instead as the subject of a case history for the elucidation of neurotic symptoms. James L. Halliday[1] becomes so engrossed in his search for the neurotic elements in Carlyle that he fails entirely to give an impression of Carlyle's literary importance—yet if it had not been for this importance no one would be spending time on Carlyle at all. The studies of Ruskin by Amabel Williams-Ellis[2] and R. H. Wilenski,[3] it should be said, are to be commended in part because of their freedom from this kind of one-sidedness.

I have not approached the authors studied here, then, as if their writings were chiefly important as providing case histories for psychiatric investigation. To make such a study, I have felt, would be to lose sight of what makes the authors significant, and to substitute detective work for literary study. But on the other hand I have tried to take account of the way personality patterns, of which significant elements are often unconscious, helped shape the author's view—for to neglect this mode of causation would lead to a one-sidedness as great as that which results from symptom-hunting. In studying Carlyle, one must keep it in mind that his was a nature beset by the most savage conflicts, that he learned in childhood to distrust his instinctive desires, that his need for authority had powerful roots in the unconscious. In studying Arnold, one must take into account the by no means morbid yet unmistakable cleavage within his personality. One can no more understand Ruskin than Carlyle without giving attention to the consequences of an imperious *super-ego* and of long-stifled instinctual drives. Study of Thomson's pessimism requires consideration of the role of neurotic guilt in his personality.

Similarly, in studying Rossetti one must form some estimate of the morbid guilt and remorse that tormented him throughout the latter part of his life. One cannot form an adequate judgment of Wilde's creativity without giving attention to the exceptional force of the principle of spontaneity in Wilde the man.

Like the psychological, the social approach—the attempt to understand an author's work by examining his way of relating himself to his society—contributes so greatly to our understanding that we cannot afford to neglect it. But this approach has its difficulties also. If the psychological approach carried to an extreme leads to symptom-hunting, the social approach carried to an extreme leads to economic determinism. The symptom-hunter is tempted to explain the author away as a case history in neurosis, and the economic determinist to explain him away as a conditioned product of the environment. The economic determinist gives the impression of failing to take account of elements of uniqueness that do not fit into economic classifications; in showing how men are shaped by their environment he loses sight of how they shape it; he appears unaware of the principle of creativity that exists in every man and is especially apparent in the major authors. In America today, however, economic determinism does not constitute a great temptation. The danger is rather that the student will permit his sense of the crudities of economic determinism to carry him to the opposite extreme and neglect, in consequence, the significant relationships between the author and his society.

But we cannot grasp Carlyle's philosophy without an appraisal of the promise and the limitations of the new social order that emerged in 1832 and of the spectacular drive of the working class between 1832 and 1848 to carry social change one step further. If we are to get at what I believe to be the essential and revealing secret of Arnold's mind, namely, the ambivalence with which he responded to the modern spirit, we must give attention both to the confidence

INTRODUCTION

of an expanding age and to the menace of violent upheaval which lasted throughout the century despite the religious revival, the new humanitarianism, and other developments making for social stabilization. In the study of Ruskin, similarly, we must give attention to such matters as the continued rift between rich and poor in the most glorious days of Victorian prosperity, the change in human motives that accompanied the growth of industrialism, and the rationalizations employed in defense of the established order. To understand Thomson's pessimism we must consider not merely his neurotic guilt but also the character of the Secularist movement with which he was identified for many years. A main key to Rossetti is the revulsion with which he responded, in common with many other men of comparable sensitivity, to the spiritual poverty, the standardization, and the hypocrisy of the mid-nineteenth century. A main key to Wilde, likewise, lies in the new social horizons that opened up during the eighties and nineties when the Victorian synthesis began to weaken.

The difficulty in studying these authors in relation to the environment lies not in avoiding the dangers of economic determinism but in getting an accurate picture of what the environment was like. The authors belong to an age in which the manufacturing and commercial classes had acquired a power and prestige they had never possessed before. The Reform Act of 1832 brought the new class to power. With the defeat of the anti-Poor Law agitation and a little later of the Chartist agitation, the manufacturers successfully prevented social change from going further than they wanted it to go. With the success of the anti-Corn Law agitation, they consolidated their gains. All the authors, then, must be considered in relation to a society whose values were increasingly shaped by the interests of manufacture and sale. But when we go further and try to get at the more exact relationship between any one of these authors and the age, the problem becomes difficult. We cannot rely exclusively on what the authors say about their own society, for if it is true that men are often unconscious of the neurotic trends that influence them, it is equally true that they may be unconscious of the way they are affected by the character of the society in which they live. Some of those who are now moving toward one variety or another of other-worldly faith, for example, whether through mystic cults or institutionalized religion, are responding to analyzable trends in our own society, but not all of them are conscious that the new interest has social as well as personal origins. The authors surveyed here, similarly, could not in the nature of things be as conscious of ways in which the environment shaped their views as we have it in our power to be. In getting at the relationship between the individual and his society, then, we cannot content ourselves merely with a reliance on the author's own testimony.

The task is to reconstruct the configuration of the environment as it affected each author, though the author may not always have been conscious of the nature of the influence. I have accordingly devoted considerable space in each essay to an account of what I believe to be the significant social patterns within which the author's thinking took shape. I have attempted in particular to bring into correct focus the one feature of Victorian society to which most histories continue to give insufficient attention, the unrest of the age. The period from 1850 to 1875 was relatively secure, but the thirties and forties were decades when men were much troubled by the threat of social upheaval, and this threat reappeared in the eighties and nineties with the emergence of modern socialism. In attempting to do justice to this feature of the age I have used, as the notes will show, some sources not generally cited in literary studies of the period. Among the books that helped me most to recapture the anxiety provoked by the menace of violent social disruption are G. D. H. Cole and Raymond Postgate, *The British Common People, 1746-1938;* Miriam Thrall, *Rebellious Fraser's;* Elie Halévy, *History of the British People: 1830-1841;* Mark Hovell, *The

Chartist Movement; J. L. and Barbara Hammond, *Lord Shaftesbury;* S. Maccoby, *English Radicalism: 1832-1852* and *English Radicalism: 1853-1886;* Frances Wentworth Knickerbocker, *Free Minds: John Morley and his Friends;* and Helen Merrell Lynd, *England in the Eighteen-Eighties: Toward a Social Basis for Freedom;* and also such contemporary books as William Rathbone Greg, *Rocks Ahead, or the Warnings of Cassandra;* Henry Mayers Hyndman, *England for All, The Record of an Adventurous Life,* and *Further Reminiscences;* Tom Mann, *Memoirs;* and E. Belfort Bax, *Reminiscences and Reflections of a Mid and Late Victorian.*

The insecurity of the age is associated with another feature to which considerable attention is given in the following studies. The Victorian age was in nothing so much like our own as in the fact that the existing form of society seemed to many men to contain within itself conflicting meanings. The age was regarded as full of promise on the one hand and of peril on the other. In so far as these authors manifest perplexity in relation to this conflict, they may be regarded as the first moderns.

In the first three chapters, we shall be concerned with three of the major social critics of the age. The key to Arnold's nature, in my opinion, lies in the way he responded to what seemed to him the almost equal force of the two opposing kinds of significance in what he called "the modern spirit." In different ways, and with different results, the thought of Carlyle and Ruskin was shaped also by the way they responded to what seemed to them opposing kinds of significance in modern society. Like these first three authors, Thomson, Rossetti and Wilde, I believe, may best be understood if their relationship to the new order of society is kept in central focus. Thomson is rightly regarded as in a sense the "classical" pessimist in English literature. Since his pessimism was in part a consequence of the breakdown of religious belief, I have occasion in the chapter on Thomson to comment on what I believe to be the significance of the torment over "loss of belief" which was so marked not only in him but in the Victorians generally. I argue here that the phenomenon is only in part a religious one, that the religious problem generally masked a social problem, though the individual concerned was likely to be unaware of the fact. Thomson, therefore, no less than Carlyle, Arnold, and Ruskin, must be understood in his relationship to the structural pattern of Victorian society. Similarly, I believe that the key to Rossetti, as to the esthetic movement of which he may be regarded as a symbol, lies in his response to the value system of the new industrial society. Wilde, finally, is related to the structure of Victorian society because he came at a moment when signs of disintegration began to appear, a moment when certain men ceased to be entrammeled by the conflict which had perplexed Arnold and others in relation to social change, but instead found themselves able to face the prospect of more complete democracy without misgivings.

When one combines the social and the psychological approach as I have attempted to do in these studies, the difficulties of the separate methods are in a sense compounded. It would be a mistake, obviously, to expect to find that in features A, B, and C an author's work will show the influence of personal conflicts while in features D, E, and F it will show the influence of the environment. One should expect an organic, not a mechanical, relationship between the two kinds of influence. The author's response to society will express itself characteristically through the mechanism of his personality and at the same time his psychological conflicts will exhibit themselves in the way he responds to his society. In the work of Thomas Wolfe, to take a recent example, to separate the study of the author's "psychology" and of his response to society would be a mistake; one must consider both aspects of Wolfe's work at the same time, for patterns of inner conflict and patterns of response to outer society were actually fused in the living author and in his work. Wolfe's "search for a father," his quest for reliable values, represented a psychological drive having its roots in childhood experience, but in adult life Wolfe's neurotic insecurity expressed itself largely in an intensification of his revolt against the established order and of the search for new patterns of social organization. Wolfe's psychological drives, that is, expressed themselves through the medium of his responses to the social environment and strengthened those responses. To take another example, Ernest Hemingway's preoccupation with virility, violence, and death is presumably a neurotic symptom in the man, whereas his comparative isolation from the practical activities of normal experience and his profound distaste for American life represent features of his mode of response to society. But the psychological and the social phenomena should not be considered separately, for the one is in part the cause of the other and has at the same time been intensified by the other.

Generally, as in these two twentieth-century authors, while we may look for priority either in the internal drives of the personality or in patterns of response to outer society, we should expect to find the two modes of activity not separate from one another but closely interrelated or even fused. We should expect, that is, an interaction between the inner dynamics of Carlyle's nature and his response to the social order inaugurated in 1832, between Arnold's psychological conflicts and his contradictory attitudes toward the democratic trends in Victorian society, between Ruskin's internal contradictions and the paradoxes in his response to the environment, between the psychological and the social causes of Thomson's pessimism, between Rossetti's neurotic symptoms and his failure in social adjustment, between Wilde's spontaneity and the creative social vision which emerged in the eighties to be reflected, at times, in his work. We should not, however, expect to find any one uniform pattern governing the interaction between social and psychological motivation in the different authors studied; to seek such a pattern would be to impose simplifying categories upon the uniqueness of individual experience.

In bringing together a psychological and a social approach to these authors I have employed a method similar to that set forth by Erich Fromm in *Studien über Autorität und Familie, Escape from Freedom,* and *Man for Himself,* and by Karen Horney in *New Ways in Psychoanalysis* and *The Neurotic Personality in Our Time.* Both are Freudian psychoanalysts, but both criticize Freud for his failure to take account of the way a particular form of society contributes to the shaping of personality patterns. Both authors give attention to the complicated ways in which psychic conditioning and a response to a particular environment interact upon one another.

These studies have largely grown out of the reading that has accompanied my teaching of the Victorian literature course at Temple University. I did not begin them with a thesis—but simply with the effort to understand certain Victorian authors. But a thesis gradually emerged: the thesis that the Victorians were the first to face a distinctively modern situation, a society that contained unbounded promise and was yet at the same time regarded by many as being full of peril, and that we can best understand the thought and spirit of these authors if we find out how in particular these two opposing responses to the modern spirit affected them.

I found myself engaged in a kind of criticism rather different, then, from the kind that is most popular today. For those critics who concern themselves little with the relationship between the author and his society but are concerned rather with the close analysis of thematic patterns and symbolic meanings in the text, I have only respect. I have the feeling, however, that one can achieve a usable understanding of an author first of all through the kind of approach I have attempted, and that the other form of criticism should come after the initial understanding has been achieved. With the Victorians the initial understanding is today what is needed.

It has often been observed that in our view of Victorian literature we lack a principle of organization. Many people look upon the phenomena of our own age without the help of a "structuralized picture of the world," as Erich Fromm has remarked. We live in a time when, for many, facts have lost "the specific quality which they can have only as parts of a structuralized whole and retain merely an abstract, quantitative meaning; each fact is just *another* fact and all that matters is whether we know more or less." Life comes to be "composed of many little pieces, each separate from the other and lacking any sense as a whole."[4] In just such a way do most of us look upon the life and literature of the Victorian period. What I am offering here is a method of structuring our understanding of the Victorian period. The approach that I have followed with these six authors would be just as serviceable, I believe, if used with most of the other Victorian authors. Macaulay, Tennyson, Swinburne, Housman, Hardy, and Morris come obviously to mind as authors who might perhaps best be understood by laying bare the relationship of each to the conflicting import of the value system of the newly established industrial society.

A thesis of the kind that has emerged from these studies obviously creates the danger of oversimplification, as every thesis does. The essays which follow will have to serve as the test of whether or not I have oversimplified the account of the six authors considered here. Clearly the way to avoid oversimplification is through fidelity to the fact. The fact, one can be safe in saying, is never simple. But what we have had in Victorian studies has been fidelity to the fact without a principle of structure, and that leads to facts without relationships, to knowledge without understanding, and to eclecticism. What is needed is fidelity to the fact plus a principle of structure. I should like to think that the principle of structure I have used here will appear sufficiently convincing so that it may serve to some degree to give pattern to one's general understanding of the Victorian period.

Of the six authors considered, the first three are among those traditionally regarded as "Victorian prophets." But in embodying certain of the characteristic features of the age, in speaking in such a way as to find a response in a large and representative body of men, in anticipating modes of experience that have followed in later times, all the authors stressed shared something of the "prophetic" character. The experience of each of them has relevance for today. In seeking to define the meaning of the experience of these authors, I have avoided, I hope, the facile morals sometimes found in nineteenth-century studies: the moral, for example, that the civilization lost its bearings because men succumbed weakly to the lure of material possessions, or the moral that the mental torment of the age had its principal source in failure to solve the problem of belief. But if I have reconstructed justly the problems these authors faced and the way they sought to solve them, the analysis attempted here should have some bearing upon the present scene; this will disclose itself, I hope, as the study proceeds.

Two

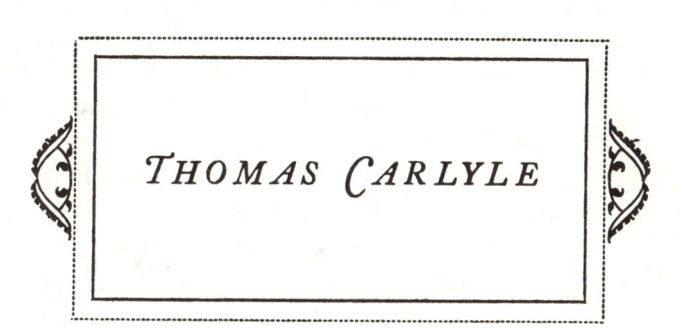

THOMAS CARLYLE

CARLYLE WAS THE FIRST TO SPEAK WITH COMMANDING ACCENTS of the social disorganization that accompanied the rise to power of the manufacturing class in the fourth decade of the nineteenth century. To this task he brought an eccentric but extraordinarily powerful style. In what he has to say about social questions one notes paradoxically both a wonderful eye for essentials and a distorting vision. The new problem Carlyle faced was that of a society with immense productive energies which it appeared powerless to direct toward humane ends. When Carlyle formulated his ideas, the factories of England were destroying men—and women and children—with a recklessness for which no precedent existed in modern times. Industrialism at the same time was bringing into being a new type of human orientation in which self-interest replaced charity, money values replaced human values, and the cash nexus replaced brotherhood as the means of relating man to man. Inherited privilege had blinded the landed class to these tragic developments; nor would this class have had the capacity or desire to correct the ills of the time if it had seen them, so preoccupied was it with the perpetuation of privilege. The manufacturing class, in spite of a philosophy professedly dedicated to "the greatest good for the greatest number," had too great a stake in the industrial order to be able to get a disinterested view of the human damage for which it was responsible. The working class was in large part too desperate to do more than struggle blindly against intolerable conditions, though soon its leaders formulated a plan of action in Chartism.

When he turned to these problems, Carlyle had already cast off institutionalized religious belief. In the nineteenth century, when the breakdown of traditional belief and painful adjustment to a world in which religious props had given way was rather the rule than the exception, loss of faith almost invariably led—as for example with Ruskin, Arnold, and Morris, as well as Carlyle—to a more earnest examination of social questions. When religion failed, the Victorians tried to construct out of the life about them a philosophy that would serve at least as a partial substitute. For Carlyle the abandonment of orthodoxy took place early in his career, not, as for so many, when he was in middle life. Later he habitually spoke with contempt of people who could not get along without their "Hebrew old clothes" but clung tenaciously to outworn dogma:

> Thirty-nine English Articles,
> Ye wondrous little particles,
> Did God shape His universe really by you?[1]

For Carlyle, as for others, the crisis in belief gave new urgency to social questions. Furthermore, because he faced social issues without dogmatic assumptions, he saw them afresh. Compelled to reject traditional ways of rationalizing man's inhumanity to man, he contemplated the agony about him as if it had never been seen, or felt, or thought about before.

But Carlyle did not, like Morris at the end of the century, construct a social philosophy independent of other-worldly sanctions. Carlyle was so insecure, he had so strong a need to be assured that the values of duty, obedience, and righteousness implanted in him in childhood had cosmic validity, that he abandoned orthodox Calvinism only to adopt a personal religion that salvaged most of Calvinism's values. His reading of German philosophy gave him the conception that a divine plan may be apprehended through intuition rather than through creeds[2] and enabled him, while rejecting traditional dogma, to keep at the center of his moral vision the belief in Providence and the moral law for which his personal insecurity created an imperious need. Transcendentalism, in a word, enabled Carlyle to forsake the catechism and yet hold on to the values the catechism had safeguarded. One of the most important of the religious values he was able to salvage in this way was the view of society as an organic community, a fellowship in which men are related to one another by ties of mutual responsibility, obligation, and trust. To be sure, his sense of the organic community had personal origins also. Though the family relationships of his childhood as they affected the unconscious sphere of the personality did incalculable damage, Carlyle's conscious memory of his family was of a closely interrelated unit where each member was interested in and responsible for the welfare of all. Carlyle's letters to his parents and to his brother John give a good impression of the psychological importance, for him, of family solidarity of this sort. Even so, Carlyle's conception of the organic society owes less to his family experience, probably, than to the way he contrived to retain, within the framework of the traditional Christian outlook, the view that men are brothers and that each is responsible for the welfare of all.

The outstanding social development of the first half of the nineteenth century was precisely the shattering of the organic society. In a time of rapid industrial expansion working people were left no choice but to take work in factories and mines under conditions of appalling horror. The act of 1802 which had restricted hours of labor for children to twelve was not enforced, and children commonly worked fourteen hours a day in factories,[3] and fourteen to sixteen hours a day in mines.[4] Such children grew up "stunted in growth, pale and sickly in appearance, and so weak as to be easy prey to diseases of the lungs and digestive organs, to distortion of the spine and deformity of the limbs."[5] This was the time when, according to current testimony, the manufacturer who would never "put his yearling colt into the shafts of his wagon, or task him with daily labor . . . yet crowds infants of six years old into his mill, confines them there, and keeps them on their feet for fifteen hours daily; while he turns their parents out of employment; and then complains of the poor-rates, and joins the chorus of lamentation about our 'surplus population.' "[6] "The agony of tortured children" in this period, Bertrand Russell has said, "is an undertone to the elegant conversation of Holland House." "Such sufferings for children," he significantly adds, "would have been impossible unless their parents had been in a condition of despair."[7] This is the period when overworked mothers used opiates—"Infant's Preservative," "Mother's Blessing," "Quietness," and "Godfrey's Cordial"— to still the cries of children they lacked strength to care for. It is the time when parents let children die so they could collect "Burial Club" insurance, as Tennyson reminds us. The Superintendent of Police in Glasgow said during the forties: "In any large block of tenements, I should be able to find a thousand children who have no name whatever, or only nicknames, like dogs."[8] G. D. H. Cole believes that working people responded to Messianic cults at this time because they were "psychologically diseased"; the need for rest, comfort, and some form of pleasure drove them to the surrogate satisfactions of prophetic religion.[9] To support the assertion that "the imagination can hardly apprehend the horror in which thousands of families a hundred years ago were born, dragged out their ghastly lives, and died," G. M. Young gives statistics as to expectation of life. In Bath, Young says, whereas a gentleman could expect to live to fifty-five, expectation of life for a laborer was twenty-five; in Derby the figure is forty-nine for the gentry and twenty-one for laborers; in Leeds, forty-five and nineteen; in Manchester, thirty-eight and seventeen; in Liverpool, thirty-five and fifteen.[10]

With these conditions the society of the time appeared unable to cope. In *The Spirit of the Age,* 1831, the young John Stuart Mill describes how the aristocracy has lost the vigor it displayed in the late seventeenth and early eighteenth centuries and now exhibits the lethargy and incompetence of inherited privilege. "Their very opinions . . . are now hereditary. Their minds were once active—they are now passive: they once generated impressions—they now merely take them. What are now their political maxims? Traditional texts, relating, directly or indirectly, to the privileges of their order, and to the exclusive fitness of men of their own sort for governing." The aristocrats, he says, have constructed an "idolatry" out of "certain abstractions . . . by dint of which they have gradually contrived, in a manner, to exclude from their minds the very idea of their living and breathing fellow-citizens, as the subjects of moral obligation in their capacity of rulers."[11] In a time when, as Bertrand Russell says, "everything needed reforming"—not only conditions of factory labor but "education, the law, the judicial system, the prisons, the insanitary condition of the towns, taxation, the Poor Law, and much else . . . the rulers of the country hunted foxes, shot pheasants, and made more stringent laws against poachers. The intelligence of the nation, as well as its humanity and common sense, rebelled against the continuation of such a system."[12]

Members of the landed class, to be sure, often denounced factory conditions, just as manufacturers denounced the exploitation of the agricultural tenantry, but to propose measures of reform was beyond their competence. Their aim was to leave things alone; they looked with suspicion on any form of social change, not only because of the inertia of privilege but because they were victims, too, of a paralyzing fear. The sound of fighting in the Paris streets following 1789 echoes in the memory throughout the nineteenth century in

England. Fearful of a similar upheaval, the aristocracy when in power before 1832 had only one remedy for the problems of the time, repressive legislation. The advocate of the mildest reform, Hesketh Pearson remarks, was labeled "Jacobin, Atheist, Incendiary, Regicide, or, as we should now term him, Bolshie."[13] The government employed spies and provocateurs to ferret out radical sentiment.[14] Cobbett fled from the threat of arrest—to publish the *Weekly Register* from the United States in 1817-18. The Peterloo Massacre of 1819 was followed by the "Six Acts," designed to destroy "seditious" protest against the existing order.

The manufacturing class which won control of the government in 1832 was very different from the landed class it superseded; it was vigorous and confident, where the landed class had been torpid and fearful. In command of the power to expand the means of production incalculably, the new class believed, with a measure of justice, that eventually the whole population would benefit from its rule. In utilitarianism the new rulers possessed a philosophy admirably calculated to win general support for policies from which the manufacturers could expect the main benefit. The utilitarian principle of "the greatest good for the greatest number"— and the reforms in balloting, law, education, and administration the Utilitarians advocated—appeared to be designed for everyone's benefit. That is why the working class, up to the time of the Reform Bill, supported the drive of the manufacturers for power.

But the new class was hardly better equipped than the aristocracy to correct the evils of industrialism. When the Reform Bill was passed the workers learned that if the Tories had been beaten, they had been beaten too.[15] The reform movement, like other movements before and since, had flown the flag of humanity to serve the ends of a class. There was a good deal more to utilitarianism, the workers soon learned, than they had foreseen. The principle of free competition by which the Utilitarians set such store, they learned, was to sanction more than the freeing of industrial enterprise from restrictions imposed by a landed class; it was to sanction also opposition to such social legislation as might curb the freedom of workers to compete with one another. Lord Brougham was soon to argue that it was a fatal blunder to regulate the labor of children, for the right to do so had been given by Providence to their parents alone.[16] While an increase in trade union activity followed immediately upon passage of the Reform Bill, it was not long before the manufacturers, discovering that unions, like factory acts, robbed the workers of their freedom, used the power of the government to oppose workers' combinations. "It is much to be regretted," says Mrs. Sparsit in *Hard Times*, "that the united masters allow of any such class-combinations."[17]

After the Reform Bill had been passed, the workers discovered the implications of the doctrines of Malthus which the Utilitarians had adopted almost to a man. Malthus gave his adherents "scientific" reasons for believing that poverty was inevitable and that there was no use, consequently, in trying to do anything about it. The new way to deal with superfluous population, an unsympathetic critic of Malthus said, was not to reclaim it but "merely to let it starve in the least objectionable way and to prevent it from having too many children."[18] When Lord Shaftesbury came before the new parliament with a plea for factory legislation, he found he could make little impression on men whose minds were "anchored in the melancholy fatalism of the new economics."[19] Malthus' doctrines, in a word, were the most vicious of those "abstract doctrines of . . . political economy" which, according to Maginn, were now "endowed with the sole control of public affairs, to the exclusion of all interference on the part of national conviction or desire."[20] To understand the widespread acceptance of Malthus' thesis, one must recall that the men who adopted it required a form of reasoning that would free them from responsibility for the wretched plight of those about them.

Even had it not been for abstract doctrines, however, the manufacturers would hardly have been in a position to correct the evils of the industrial system, for competition at home and abroad compelled them to resist every measure that would increase costs. Althorp spoke for his whole class when he warned in parliament that Lord Shaftesbury's factory legislation would weaken Britain's ability to compete with other countries in manufacture.[21] The House of Commons, Cobbett said, had concluded that the strength of England lay not in her navy, not in her commerce, not in her colonies, but in the labor of thirty thousand little girls.[22] The new masters of England were the men who in *Hard Times* complained that "they were ruined, when they were required to send laboring children to school; they were ruined, when inspectors were appointed to look into their works; they were ruined, when such inspectors considered it doubtful whether they were quite justified in chopping people up with their machinery; they were utterly undone, when it was hinted that perhaps they need not always make quite so much smoke."[23] They were men compelled by economic necessity to sacrifice humane scruples to the motive of economic gain, as Dickens again reminds us when he says that Bitzer showed weakness in allowing his mother half a pound of tea a year, "first, because all gifts have an inevitable tendency to pauperize the recipient, and secondly, because his only reasonable transaction in the commodity would have been to buy it for as little as he could possibly give, and sell it for as much as he could possibly get; it having been clearly ascertained by philosophers that in this is comprised the whole duty of man—not a part of man's duty, but the whole."[24]

Almost immediately after the Reform Bill was passed, the working class, which up to that time had been allied with the manufacturers in the struggle against aristocracy, began to contend with the new governing class. To this new struggle the workers transferred the revolutionary energy they had previously brought to the reform agitation. Working-class pressure, one recalls, had been largely responsible for passage of the Reform Bill, for it was the threat of civil disorder reminiscent of 1789 that persuaded the Tories to yield. There had been riots in Bristol and London; Nottingham Castle was burned, Derby gaol was sacked.[25] Francis Place was organizing the resort to arms that might be necessary if the Tories refused to give way.[26] Carlyle, among others, believed that an intransigeant parliament might provoke armed rebellion.[27] When the battle was won, however, the workers received their reward in the New Poor Law of 1834. The aim of the new law, it appeared, was to make the only available relief less desirable than the worst employment and so to place the working people at the mercy of their employers. Relief was now to be given only to the occupants of poor houses—the "Bastilles," as they came to be called—where conditions were designedly as atrocious as was appropriate for the poor at a time when money was becoming a proof of virtue and the lack of it evidence of a depraved character. Now began the agitation against the three "tyrants" or "Pashas" of the Poor Law Commission,[28] an agitation soon to be followed by the mighty campaign for the People's Charter. The two working-class movements of the thirties and forties, the anti-Poor Law agitation and Chartism, were directed against the manufacturers. In the fifteen or twenty years after the Reform Bill, says G. D. H. Cole, the opposition between middle class and working class "was more universally taken to be the key to current history than it has ever been since or before except perhaps in twentieth-century Russia."[29]

The manufacturing class now began to manifest a fear of social change comparable to that of the aristocracy in the days before the Reform Bill. To be sure, the new governing class still had battles to fight for its own freedom—the battle against the Corn Laws, in particular. But henceforth the conflict between manufacturers and aristocracy, though real, was subordinated in a tacit agreement. The danger for the manufacturers now was not so much obstruction on the right as militancy on the left. Earlier, when the aristocracy had been filled with horror by the French Revolution, the manufacturers had shared something of their fear but had felt also a stirring of radical ambitions as they foresaw the possibility of revolt against the restraints imposed upon them by the landed class. After 1832 the manufacturers had little to gain through social change, but in view of the militancy growing out of the desperate plight of the working class, they had much to fear. Now the manufacturers, like the aristocracy before them, turned to repressive measures. They tried at the same time to educate the workers as to the benefits of the factory system. Lord Brougham founded the Society for the Diffusion of Useful Knowledge—the "Steam Intellect Society"—to "preach thrift," in the words of William Morris, "to (precarious) incomes of eighteen shillings a week, and industry to men killing themselves by inches working overtime, or to men whom the labor-market [had] rejected as not wanted,"[30] and to advise workers that restraint in begetting children would serve better than unions as a means of improving their conditions.[31]

These were the conditions Carlyle confronted when he turned to social criticism. To his task he brought the freshness of view of a man who has discarded the traditional religious outlook, plus a determination to discover whatever significance the practices of his society might have for one who was constructing a social philosophy intended, like religion, to reveal ultimate meanings. He brought the conviction, originating in family upbringing and strengthened by transcendentalism, that society must be regarded as a human fellowship or communion. He brought a superlatively emphatic literary style. With this equipment he developed his great moral critique of a new world situation, for the industrial conditions in England in the first half of the nineteenth century were soon to be reproduced, in their main features at least, throughout the greater part of the world.

Carlyle assailed both governing classes for the way they had abdicated responsibility. His excoriation of the aristocracy of idlers was more stinging than Mill's, for it was winged with a savagery whose sources lay in his tortured personality. "We have private individuals whose wages are equal to the wages of seven or eight thousand other individuals. What do these highly beneficed individuals *do* to society for their wages? — *Kill partridges.* CAN this last? No, by the soul that is in man it cannot, and will not, and shall not."[32] More important, Carlyle developed the classic criticism of the apologists for a social order that subordinates human to money values. He carried to the wide audience his force of style won for him the views expressed in William Maginn's condemnation of those who had taught themselves to "think of nothing but the 'wealth' of nations; to look at the balance-sheet of imports and exports, and to judge from that of the prosperity of the country; to examine the quantity of the goods produced, without bestowing a thought upon the producer; and to think that the strength of a nation consists not in well-affected hearts and valiant hands, but in the figures which tell that so much cotton was imported, so much iron exported, so many power-looms erected, so many small farms devastated to be thrown into larger ones. . . . A shilling saved is sufficient reason for consigning our fellow-citizens to beggary."[33] "No sect in our day," Carlyle said, "has made a wretcheder figure than the Bentham Radical sect . . . a wretched, unsympathetic, scraggy Atheism and Egoism."[34] Political economy could be a useful science, he conceded, "but so is a cow useful"; to permit the science of barter to provide us with notions of human welfare was to "put the cow in the parlor."[35] The rule of life men need is one that tells them "by what causes men are happy, moral, religious, or the contrary," but the rule of life we have adopted "tells us how 'flannel jackets' are exchanged for 'pork hams,' and speaks much about 'the land last taken into cultivation.' " The political economists "are the hodmen of the intellectual edifice, who have got upon the wall and will insist on building as if they were masons."[36]

The traditional Christian conception of man's duty to man was being replaced, in Carlyle's view, by a new conception by contrast incredibly limited and mean. Selflessness as an ideal of conduct was giving way to self-advantage. Acquisitiveness was being transformed from a vice into a virtue. Painting unforgettable pictures of the hopeless faces of the Bastilles, he compelled his readers to take account of the human degradation for which industrialism was responsible. He derided the glorification of commercial success. "Gigmanity," he said—veneration for the man who is able to own a gig—was "the Baal worship of our time."[37] He was the first to describe the insufficiency of a society in which men were related to one another only by the cash nexus. "We have *no communion*," he said; "company enough, but no fellowship."[38] As a step toward restoring communion he proposed that each man should begin to assume a share of responsibility for the general welfare and that the government abandon laissez faire and take steps to alleviate the plight of society's victims. Speaking of Shaftesbury's proposals for factory legislation, he said that "the Government were absolutely bound either to try whether they could do some good to these people, or to draw them out in line and openly shoot them with grape."[39] He complained to Emerson about "the selfish abdication of public men of all that public persons should perform." Paupers from Ireland, he said, came wandering over the moors in Scotland. Mrs. Carlyle feeds them, "but there are thousands of acres which might give them all meat, and nobody to bid these poor Irish go to the moor and till it."[40]

These views Carlyle expressed with such power as to gain an instant hearing. "To the young, the generous, to everyone who took life seriously, who wished to make an honorable use of it, and could not be content with sitting down and making money, his words were like the morning reveille."[41] The conditions he assailed lasted in essentials throughout the century, but no one after Carlyle could confront them without having his response influenced to some degree by what Carlyle had written. When William Morris visited a group of socialists in Glasgow late in the century, he noted that most of them gave credit to Carlyle for having exercised a decisive influence on their thinking.[42]

Carlyle's indictment of the civilization of his day is invaluable, but when he went further and spoke not merely about what was wrong but about where men should look for help, he developed a philosophy that has since been discredited everywhere, except among certain followers of Hitler and Mussolini a few years ago. Among those who suffered most from the disorders of expanding industrialism, it is important to remember, many had no hesitation about the remedy; but the remedy they proposed was of a kind that Carlyle was unable to adopt. They believed that the political changes that had put the new class in power should be not halted but continued and used as an instrument to modify the industrial system sufficiently to free the workers from factory slavery. Owenism was widely diffused among working people before and after the Reform Bill. Robert Owen, persuaded that the profit system itself meant inevitable misery for the masses, advocated coöperative enterprise. Leaders of the trade-union movement, which expanded rapidly after repeal of the Combination Acts in 1824, and still more rapidly in the first years after the Reform Bill, were many of them Owenites. Those who organized the Grand Consolidated Trades Union in 1834 were committed to Owen's principles,[43] as was William Lovett, the leader of the London Working Men's Association, who argued that the evils of the day had their source in the institution of private property itself, and proposed to work through education and political action toward a coöperative commonwealth.[44] For Henry Hetherington, another leader of the London Working Men's Association, also an Owenite, the evil to be extirpated was nothing less than the "competitive, scrambling, selfish system" itself, "a system in which the moral and social aspirations of the noblest human being are nullified by incessant toil and physical deprivations: by which indeed all men are trained to be either slaves, hypocrites, or criminals."[45]

Like the trade-unionists, the leaders of the two mass agitations of the thirties and forties, the struggle against the Poor Law and Chartism, had clear ideas also as to how the problems of the working people should be solved, but their solution too was one that Carlyle could not accept. To be sure, the mass support for these movements came from men who sought blindly any kind of redress of grievances and had no well-considered ideas as to the direction which social or political change might desirably take. Their sanctions were often religious rather than economic or political, for a "religious sanction for radical opinions is the only refuge for persons unacquainted with abstract political, or social or economic theory," as Hovell says.[46] The leaders of the two movements, however, had clear ideas as to how political democracy might be used as an instrument of social regeneration.[47] The six points of the Charter were political, but the Chartist leaders intended to use political power for economic ends.

Penetrating as was Carlyle's analysis of the shortcomings of the existing order, he could not, like the mass leaders of the time, seek a remedy in the extension of democracy. To understand why Carlyle could not take the step that seemed logical to many of his contemporaries, and to understand the antidemocratic philosophy he erected on a perfectly sound critical base, one must take into consideration the way the conflicts of his tormented nature influenced his thinking.

One is struck immediately in Carlyle's work by symptoms of intense anxiety. "I spent an evening at Carlyle's some fortnight since," writes Herbert Spencer. "He is a queer creature; and I should soon be terribly bored with him were I long in his company. His talk is little else than a continued tirade against the 'horrible, abominable state of things.' He was very bitter against the Exhibition, among other things, and was very wroth at the exposure to the public of such disgusting brutes as the monkeys at the Zoological Gardens."[48] "With his constitutional tendency to antagonism, and his unmeasured assumption of superiority," Spencer says in summarizing his impression of Carlyle, "he was ever finding occasion to scorn and condemn and denounce. . . . He had a daily secretion of curses which he had to vent on somebody or something."[49] Harriet Martineau was of the opinion that Carlyle's savagery in speech had its source in an "intolerable sympathy with suffering" which constituted the "master-pain" of his life.[50] Today one can have little doubt, however, that this verbal aggression had its source in neurotic repression.

Another indication of psychic maladjustment in Carlyle lies in the way he repeatedly fell victim to states of morbid depression. "My thoughts lie around me all inarticulate, sour, fermenting, bottomless, like a hideous enormous bog of Allan," he would write, "a thing ugly, painful, of use to no one."[51] "I seem to myself at present, and for a long while past, to be sunk deep, fifty miles deep, below the region of articulation, and, if I ever rise to speak again, must raise whole continents with me."[52] Here the metaphor itself discloses the subconscious sources of the malady, as it does when on another occasion he exclaims that he was "never in [his] life nearer *sunk* in the mud oceans that rage from within and without,"[53] and yet again when he exclaims: "O God, it is a fearful world, this we live in, a film spread over bottomless abysses, into which no eye has pierced."[54] (One notes the aptness with which the metaphor here suggests the neurotic's fear of the "bottomless abysses" of the unconscious self.) Exclamations like these were torn from Carlyle at times when he suffered, as he did periodically throughout his life, from a state of paralysis of the will, hopelessness, self-commiseration, and despair. Such moods were accompanied by a dread of unknown perils: "Why is the past so beautiful?" he asks, and then answers, "The element of *fear* is withdrawn from it for one thing. That is all safe, while the present and future are all so dangerous."[55] These moods were accompanied too by the sense of being shut out from the community, for Carlyle complained repeatedly in his journals of his "silence and isolation, [his] utter loneliness in this world."[56] From these states of dejection he tried valiantly to wrest himself. "Ah me! or, rather: Courage! Courage!" he exclaims.[57] And again: "I fear not the world. What are its frowns or its favors? What are its difficulties and falsehoods and hollow threatenings to me? With the spirit of my father I will front and conquer them."[58]

The dyspepsia from which Carlyle suffered—and which he treated by castor oil in triple doses—was almost unquestionably a physical symptom of neurosis.[59] If further evidence of personal maladjustment were needed, one might refer to the sexual dysfunction which even an age most hesitant to disclose intimate facts about great men proved unable to conceal. Whether or not Froude was justified in his belief that Carlyle's was a marriage "only in name,"[60] there is no question that the disorder of his personality was severe enough to affect the sphere of sexuality.

If a psychiatrist had examined Carlyle in 1824, James L. Halliday says, the diagnosis would have run something like this: "This is a compulsive 'anal character' of high intelligence, and with definite paranoid traits of inflation and self-isolation, marked sadistic and masochistic tendencies, and schizoid features. He is very egocentric and narcissistic and suffers from periodical phases of depression and passivity when he is disciplined to do anything. He shows much self-pity, helplessness, self-reproach and ideas of unworthiness. He has a hypochondriacal preoccupation with his gastro-intestinal tract. When his depressions lift he becomes productive —almost hypomanic and even grandiose. There is probably some relation between the serious disorder of his personality and his gastric complaints whose onset occurred six years ago when his social environment was unsatisfactory—as it still is. He apparently had a serious breakdown almost psychotic in nature two years ago."[61] Halliday suggests possible causes of the repression and conflict in Carlyle's nature by reconstructing his early relationship with his parents. Later in life Carlyle displayed an excessive attachment to his mother and something like veneration for his father. In early infancy, Halliday conjectures, Carlyle may have been driven by fear of abandonment to adopt his mother's views of right and wrong, the direct opposite of his instinctive desires. His early response to his father, Halliday believes, was probably one of terror and hatred, but he thinks that in order to gain security Carlyle developed toward his father a conscious attitude of affection and obedience. Here would be two causes, then, of conflict and repression. The spiritual crisis related in *Sartor Resartus*, in Halliday's opinion, culminated in an experience of mystic union with the father, in which Carlyle sought once and for all to submerge his hostility by making his father's nature completely his own.

The objection to Halliday's book, as was mentioned earlier, is that the author becomes so absorbed in psychoanalyzing Carlyle that he gives little more than lip service to Carlyle's significance as a literary figure. The book is not open to objection, as are some psychoanalytical studies of authors long dead, on the ground that sufficient evidence is lacking, with the result that the biographer must build his case out of guesswork rather than fact. Concerning Carlyle's neurotic nature an abundance of evidence is available. To be sure, Halliday must resort to conjecture when he speaks of the infantile origins of neurosis, but even here his conjectures are guarded and plausible.

Those who may not be prepared to adopt the conceptual framework of Halliday's analysis will hardly question that Carlyle conforms closely to the account of the authoritarian character given by Erich Fromm. The authoritarian character, according to Fromm's analysis, erects in childhood a powerful principle of authority—the *super-ego* or conscience—to aid in the repression of instinctual drives which have come to be regarded as a menace to security. Such a person is torn by incessant conflicts between instinctual drives and the tyrannical *super-ego* which forbids their expression. Men of this sort, regarding values approved by the *super-ego* as "good" and the impulses associated with the *id* as "evil," come to be preoccupied, in their thinking about themselves and about others, with questions of right and wrong. Feeling that only the most rigorous authority can restrain or repress the anarchic forces within, they often come to believe that society in general is in need of a comparable principle of authority. Sensitive as they are to the "danger" of instinctual drives, they come to feel that the self-assertion of the masses represents a similar danger to society generally. The inner experience of such persons is not one of the activity of harmonious powers, of emotion freely expressing itself under the guidance of reason, as in a character of strong *ego* development; it is an experience, rather, of fierce revolt and fiercer repression, of approval and disapproval, of dominance and subjection. Such persons almost invariably come to feel that the relationship between man and man has a similar character. "The authoritarian character may sometimes use the word equality . . . because it suits his purposes. But it has no real meaning or weight for him, since it concerns something outside the reach of his emotional experience. For him the world is composed of people with power and those without it, of superior ones and inferior ones. . . . He experiences only domination or submission, but never solidarity. Differences, whether of sex or race, to him are necessarily signs of superiority or inferiority. A difference which does not have this connotation is unthinkable to him."[62]

The authoritarian character is constantly menaced by the danger that suppressed drives will force their way to the surface and shatter the precarious balance of the personality. He responds by strengthening the interior authority, only to be beset by an intangible sense of impending calamity. This sense he often projects upon society, so that he comes to feel that his times are "full of peril" and that social disaster is imminent. A characteristic means through which such a person wards off anxiety is through compulsive activity — through work. "The state of anxiety, the feeling of powerlessness and insignificance . . . represent a state of mind which is practically unbearable. . . . One possible way to escape this unbearable state of uncertainty and the paralyzing feeling of one's insignificance is the very trait which became so prominent in Calvinism: the development of frantic activity and a striving to do something. . . . This kind of effort and activity is not the result of inner strength and self-confidence; it is a desperate escape from anxiety."[63]

This analysis of the authoritarian character provides us with our best clue to the reactionary philosophy which Carlyle constructed on the basis of clear-sighted social perceptions, for in him appears every one of the traits that Fromm enumerates. When Carlyle compared existing society with his own conception of the organic human community, he was able to show how the age had lost its bearings, but when he confronted the proposal that these conditions be corrected through an extension of democracy, the dynamic of the authoritarian character intervened. He felt pity enough for the dazed and bewildered victims of the system, but when he contemplated the possibility that the problem might be solved through the self-assertion of great masses of men he was overwhelmed by the sense that to release these drives would be as dangerous and iniquitous as to give free rein to the drives of his own instinctual nature. To continue the political revolution, he concluded, was the one way not to solve the problem, for "revolution meant only the letting of the devil loose, whom it was man's duty to keep bound."[64] Any proposal to enlarge the area wherein man might seek fulfillment of his instinctive or emotional nature aroused in Carlyle irrational revulsion. He speaks of the "mangy hungry discontent" of Mill's friends,[65] and is horrified by their advocacy of easier divorce laws.[66] He will have nothing to do with the new and more tolerant attitude toward the criminal. Many would now regard as one of the more creative developments of the nineteenth century the tendency, reflected later in Samuel Butler's *Erewhon* and in William Morris's *News from Nowhere*, to view crime as a disease and to devise ways to rehabilitate the criminal rather than punish him; but Carlyle could no more approve the attempt to approach the criminal with an uncensorious effort to understand him than he could approve a similar approach to the instinctive drives of his own nature. The way to treat instinctive drives, he felt, was to repress them; the way to treat the criminal was to throw him in jail.

To advocate a democratic solution to the problems of the time required trust in people, but Carlyle as an authoritarian character was incapable of trust. He could approve or disapprove, revere or contemn, but he had no confidence that people might by their own efforts be able to find the right way to solve their own problems. Increasingly, as a matter of fact, his attitude toward ordinary people became one of contempt; approval and reverence were kept for the leaders of men, while disapproval and condemnation were directed against the followers. He speaks of a "blockhead" who complained to him that "we're very ill governed." "He that would govern you well would surprise you much, my friend," Carlyle retorts, "laying a hearty horsewhip on that back of yours."[67] When Ruskin became chairman of the committee to defend Governor Eyre, Carlyle described the event in language that makes very clear the combination of aggression and contempt that characterized his attitude toward ordinary human nature: "Impetuous Ruskin," he said, "plunges his rapier up to the hilt in the abominable belly of the vast blockheadism, and leaves it staring very considerably."[68] When Emerson gave lectures at Mechanics' Institutes, Carlyle remarked that he was addressing himself "in fact, though he knows it not, to a kind of intellectual *canaille*."[69] The public which welcomed his *Cromwell* he dismissed as "poor bewildered blockheads."[70] He was less and less able to interest himself in the rights of the people, in short, as he became more and more impressed with their imbecility.[71] "The immense mass of men he believed to be poor creatures, poor in heart and poor in intellect, incapable of making any progress at all if left to their own devices, though with a natural loyalty, if not distracted into self-conceit, to those who were wiser and better than themselves. . . . So far from being able to guide or govern themselves, their one chance of improvement lay in their submitting to their natural superiors, whether by their free will or else by compulsion."[72]

Those who advocated a democratic solution to the problems of the time urged broader political representation as an instrument through which their ends might be achieved, but the authoritarian dynamic in Carlyle engendered in him such contempt for ordinary men that he came to look on the parliamentary process itself as vain. The parliamentary process, he believed with Tanner in *Man and Superman,* meant substitution of "election by the incompetent many" for "appointment by the corrupt few."[73] "Most weary, flat, stale, seem to me all the electioneerings, the screechings, and jibberings, that the earth is filled with, in these, or indeed in any days."[74] These words represent well the tone with which Carlyle habitually speaks of political democracy. Carlyle was right when he pointed out that the blessings of political freedom in nineteenth-century England were not so great as was sometimes implied, that to be free as factory workers were free was not much to be preferred to slavery;[75] for the conditions had now emerged which led Shaw later to declare that human slavery "has reached its worst recorded point within our own time in the form of free wage labor."[76] But his opposition to the parliamentary process was motivated less by his grasp of the way economic slavery was robbing political freedom of its meaning than by the conviction that ordinary men were no more competent to make intelligent decisions about their welfare than were the spontaneous impulses of the personality capable in themselves of achieving harmony and ordered purpose.

In talking about parliamentary procedures Carlyle made great use of analogies drawn from navigation, agriculture, and medicine. There was a right way of doing things and a wrong way, he would aver, and "it was as foolish to suppose that the *right* way of managing the affairs of a nation could be ascertained by a majority of votes, as the right way of discovering the longitude, of cultivating the soil, of healing diseases, or of exercising any one of the million arts on which our existence and welfare depend."[77] It was as sensible to decide national affairs by the ballot as for a ship's crew to use the ballot to determine the right course.[78] Carlyle was capable of seeing, if he had wished to see it, the fallacy that has often enough been pointed out in this analogy—the fallacy that has its source in neglect of the distinction between areas of experience where each man has something pertinent to say about his welfare and other areas of experience where technical knowledge is indispensable. It was not inability to make this distinction but the authoritarian character's conviction that men must be kept in their place through repressive discipline that led Carlyle to speak of the "creed of liberty, equality, and government by majority of votes" as "the most absurd superstition which had ever bewitched the human imagination—at least, outside Africa."[79]

Social stability, Carlyle came to believe, could be maintained only as his personal stability was maintained from day to day, through force. "If people would not behave," Margaret Fuller quotes Carlyle as saying, "put collars round their necks."[80] Again, just as personal stability required a strong *super-ego*, so social stability, Carlyle came to believe, required an impregnable center of authority, a leader or hero. The science of government, he said, was to find the best man and to raise him to kingship. When he spoke of "the everlasting worth, dignity, and blessedness of work,"[81] again, Carlyle was introducing into his social philosophy a belief that had its source in his psychological make-up—in the compulsive activity, in this instance, through which he defended himself against neurotic anxiety.

One should not assume that Carlyle's psychic nature made his social theory inevitable. One's views about society are no more mechanically determined by the dynamics of the personality than they are by class, nationality, or climate. If certain circumstances had been different, Carlyle might well have evolved a democratic philosophy in spite of the authoritarian tendencies developed early in his nature. If he had found warm and secure personal relationships, he might have become a more balanced individual, and the psychological change might well have modified his social theory. If the advocates of democratic change had possessed a firmer, more explicit program, one free from the insurrectionary threat of Chartism, he might have been able to find a way to join them. If he had lived in the age of psychoanalysis, he might have been assisted to resolve the conflicts that impelled him toward authoritarian attitudes—though one must admit that, judging from the experience of our own time, the psychiatrists would very likely have encouraged him to forget the plight of humanity and take up golf. These conditions, however, were lacking, and in their absence it appears clear that it was personal character structure rather than German philosophy or any other influence that led Carlyle to adopt an antidemocratic solution to the problems of his age.

The philosophy Carlyle developed was not stable. The authoritarian means of solving personal conflict solves nothing permanently. The conflicts and the resulting anxiety remain, and the need to escape to work, the need perpetually to reaffirm the principle of authority, remain with them. Much the same was true of Carlyle's social philosophy. He looked constantly for a "hero" who would put the common man in his place, but no such leader emerged; meanwhile the self-assertion of the masses continued to generate in the body politic a tension comparable to the tension created within the personality by the self-assertion of instinctive forces. It was primarily because his social philosophy was one that failed to offer anything resembling a stable or permanent solution to the problem with which it dealt that Carlyle was thrown back constantly to the conviction that humanity can be saved only through individual reform. "Vain hope to make mankind happy by politics! You cannot drill a regiment of knaves into a regiment of honest men, enregiment and organize them as cunningly as you will. Give us the honest men, and the well-ordered regiment comes of itself. Reform one man—reform thy own inner man; it is more than scheming for a nation."[82] Occasionally, it is true, Carlyle does advocate specific change in social structure through legislative measures—repeal of the Corn Laws, factory reform, certain modifications of laissez faire, as in *Past and Present*. But generally he insists that the only kind of change that has meaning is a change in the individual heart. "For the sick body and sick soul of modern Europe there was but one remedy, the old remedy of the Jewish prophets, repentance and moral amendment. All men, high and low, wise and unwise, must call back into their minds the meaning of the word 'duty'; must put away their cant and hypocrisy, their selfishness and appetite for pleasure, and speak truth and justice. Without this, all tinkering with the constitution . . . would avail nothing."[83] As much as any thinker of the nineteenth century Carlyle believed that social regeneration was to be brought about by personal reform rather than, as the twentieth century is often inclined to see it, personal reform through social regeneration.

Carlyle's invectives against the Mammonism of his contemporaries were not designed to alter the conditions which impelled men to put stress on money values, but merely to fortify the individual in his effort to resist the materialism of the day. Similarly he urged an extension of popular education, not because he regarded education as a means toward changes in the structure of society, but because he regarded it as a means toward change in the individual spirit. To be sure, this stress on the individual is of the essence of traditional Christianity—it was one of the features of orthodoxy that Carlyle's transcendentalism preserved and reinforced. One may judge from his Rectorship Address delivered at Edinburgh University in 1866 how close Carlyle's message came to religious truism; he told the undergraduates that they should lead good lives, not care too much for worldly success, and leave the rest to Providence. No doubt this personal appeal was attractive to Carlyle also because it implied a flat refutation of the views held by men like the Chartists, who believed that "tinkering with the constitution" was far from fruitless. But it was primarily the instability of his social philosophy that impelled Carlyle to fall back on an appeal for individual reform. When John Stuart Mill spoke in *The Spirit of the Age* of the hopelessness of trying to effect social change by reforming individuals,[84] he showed how different was the direction of his own thinking from Carlyle's.

To what features of Carlyle's thinking should one attribute the great influence he exerted on the conscience of his time? It is worth noting, perhaps, that authoritarianism was a part of the character structure of his age. Traits that appeared in exaggerated form in Carlyle were present in some degree in most men. The aim of the schools throughout the nineteenth century was not what Sydney Smith said it should be and what in the best schools it later became, to free the child from "every species of useless vexation" and grant him "in the greatest degree, the blessings of a wise and rational indulgence."[85] It was rather to develop within the pupil a center of authority that would enable him to crush the appetites of the natural man. Men so trained were understandably more receptive to a philosophy like Carlyle's than men reared in a democratic environment would have been. But the real secret of Carlyle's influence lies in the fact that with great literary power he awoke people to the magnitude of the social issues of the time, and then set before them a philosophy that counterbalanced its ineffectuality by the advantage of being morally safe. The doctrine of work, glorification of the hero, distrust of the political aims of the common man, insistence that reform must start with the individual—this was a message gladly received by men who feared a democratic solution to the problems of the day.

Carlyle's attack on the do-nothing aristocracy should not mislead one into thinking that he offered any real threat to the status of the landed class. Even in the eighteen-thirties Carlyle's view, as we have seen, was close to the Tory views propounded in *Fraser's Magazine* by William Maginn.[86] The radicalism of the young Carlyle had many points in common with that of Oastler and Stephens, leaders of the anti-Poor Law movement,[87] of Michael Sadler, parliamentary opponent of laissez faire,[88] of Lord Shaftesbury, and of the young Disraeli—all of whom, like William Maginn, were Tories. As time went on, Carlyle drew closer to the aristocracy. As tutor to the Buller family, he had been impressed mainly by the emptiness and ennui of upper-class lives,[89] but as his friendship grew with Lord and Lady Ashburton he was more and more impressed by the polish, wit, and splendor of the aristocracy. He came to regard the Ashburton household much as Sydney Smith regarded Holland House when he wrote that "it was . . . an enchanted palace, where wit and beauty reigned supreme, where the art of feeding and drinking was practised to perfection, where liberal sentiments and faultless breeding were in exquisite harmony, and where civilization had reached its apogee."[90] Of a dinner at the Ashburtons' Carlyle writes: "Their art in speech, more and more noticeable gradually, is decidedly a thing to be considered valuable, venerable. Real good breeding, as the people have it here, is one of the finest things now going on in the world. The careful avoidance of all discussion, the swift hopping from topic to topic, does not agree with me; but the graceful skill they do it with is beyond that of minuets."[91] In 1823 Carlyle had been able to sum up his view of the aristocracy with the remark: "Had the parties all wrapped themselves in warm blankets and kept their beds, much peace had been among several hundreds of his Majesty's subjects, and the same result, the uneasy destruction of half-a-dozen hours, had been quite as well attained. . . . There is something in the life of a sturdy peasant toiling from sun to sun for a plump wife and six eating children; but as for the Lady Jerseys and the Lord Petershams, peace be with them."[92] But in the *Reminiscences,* published in 1881, the view had changed: "Certain of the Aristocracy, however, did seem to me still very *noble;* and, with due elimination of the grossly worthless . . . I should vote at present that, of *classes* known to me in England, the Aristocracy (with its perfection of human politeness, its continual grace of bearing and of acting, steadfast 'honor,' light address and cheery stoicism, if you see *well* into it), is actually yet the best of English Classes."[93]

Yet paradoxically it was the new manufacturing class, the class he denounced with such vehemence, that most greatly benefited from Carlyle's influence. One must not be misled by the acerbity of Carlyle's attack on the profit-and-loss economy and the Mammonism of the commercial classes. The leaders of the industrial society of Carlyle's time were prepared to accept almost any amount of criticism on the score of their materialism; for some of them, it may be, such criticism served to allay a sense of guilt. But what the new class most greatly needed was a way to forestall the demand that social change be continued in the direction of fuller democracy. In evolving a social philosophy that appeared to take full account of the crisis of the time and that not only did not call for, but opposed, this kind of solution, Carlyle performed a service for the new governing class that far outweighed his tirades against the "scraggy Atheism and Egoism" of the "Bentham Radical sect."

Three

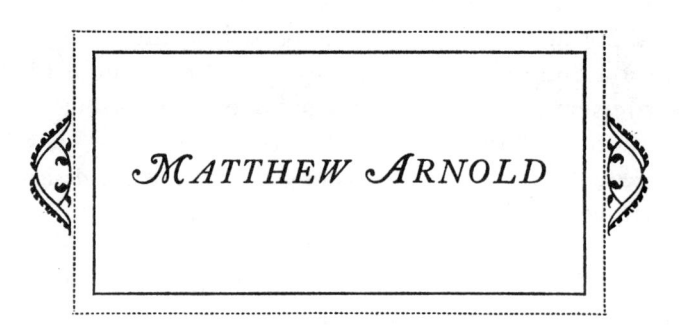

MATTHEW ARNOLD

COMPARED WITH CARLYLE, MATTHEW ARNOLD WAS A MAN whose inner nature was strongly integrated. His mind and his feelings were, compared with Carlyle's, free. He was sufficiently in command of his inner self to be able to cultivate the art of living as William Morris understood the term, to be able, that is, to bring undivided attention and interest to the ordinary occurrences of everyday life. His letters abound in instances of a capacity for relaxed enjoyment that Carlyle never knew: "I have just been out with Lucy and Nelly to clear some superfluous apricots from the trees. We gather a stray strawberry or two, but they have not done well this year, and we shall have but few. Then there has been an alarm of the pigs in the garden and there were the pretty little fellows trotting about among the beds. They are so small that they can get through the iron fence when let out into the field, and they must not be let out till they are bigger. The whole family has been engaged in driving them back, and with much laughter this has at last been accomplished."[1]

Yet many signs show that integration did not come effortlessly to Arnold. He was one of those who constantly make resolutions bearing upon the conduct of day-to-day life: "I am getting more of a distinct feeling as to what I want to read; however, this, though a great step, is not enough without strong command over oneself to make oneself follow one's rule; conviction, as the Westminster divines say, must precede conversion, but does not imply it."[2] He made constant use of the capsuled reflections on the art of living provided by maxim-writers—Eugénie and Maurice de Guérin, Joubert, Emerson, Goethe, Marcus Aurelius. "A life without a purpose is a languid, drifting thing." "Always place a definite purpose before thee." "Get the habit of mastering thine inclination." "Not frequently nor without necessity to say to anyone, or to write in a letter, that I have no leisure; nor continually to excuse the neglect of duties required by our relation to those with whom we live, by alleging urgent occupation." For the man who stored up for his own use maxims of this sort, the conduct of life was not entirely a simple thing. Arnold was not compelled perpetually to win victories over his instinctive nature, as Carlyle was, but he was one of those nevertheless for whom the effort to achieve inner harmony requires constant attention.

Arnold's poems give abundant evidence of his consciousness of a rift within his own nature and of his effort to achieve and re-achieve unity. Many of the poems may be regarded, to borrow Kenneth Burke's phrase,[3] as "strategies" for achieving a balance between opposed forces of mind and spirit. A recurrent theme in the poetry, for instance, is the conflict between feeling and intellect, spontaneity and control. The true life for the poet, Arnold believed, as did the romantic poets, was that of the feelings. In poems like "Quiet Work," "Indifference," "The Youth of Man," and "Self-Dependence," he makes it clear that the ideal existence must have in it something of the spontaneity he associates with nature; to live this life, we must be freed somehow from the "hourly false control" of the intellect. Arnold agreed with Wordsworth that poetry had its source in spontaneous delight. Yet he knew at the same time that if he was not to forfeit that quality of seriousness which alone could enable poetry to fulfill its grand function as *magister vitae*,[4] he must be faithful to the demands of the intellect. The life of the intellect and the life of the feelings, however, appeared incompatible. We must be true to the reason, he wrote in a penciled note to "Obermann Once More," or we shall perish as the Romans did: "What really wounds and perplexes me," he then added, is that "the service of reason is freezing to feeling, chilling to the religious mood," and "feeling and the religious mood," he noted, "are eternally the deepest being of men, the ground of all joy and greatness in him."[5]

The cleavage appears in other guises—the variety of its manifestations being an indication, perhaps, that Arnold himself was not fully aware of its meaning. It appears, for example, in the opposition between youth and age. He contrasts the "glad, perennial youth" of the Scholar Gipsy with the fatigue, weariness, and resignation of those who have resigned themselves to the world's sway. Youth, he says in "The Progress of Poetry," is the time for poetic creation; age develops the intellect but dries up the springs of inspiration. "The aimless and unsettled, but also open and liberal state of our youth," he writes, "we must perhaps all leave and take refuge in our morality and character; but with most of us it is a melancholy passage from which we emerge shorn of so many beams that we are tempted to quarrel with the law of nature which imposes it on us."[6] It was because he associated youth with spontaneity and age with the chilling action of the intellect, perhaps, that Arnold was so sensitive to the theme of mutability and spoke of the coming on of age—when he was not yet forty—as a calamity.

The conflict appears again in the opposition between the claims of a freely imaginative or passionate existence on the one hand and the claims of society and conformity on the other. "The Forsaken Merman" contrasts a world of imagination "where the salt weed sways in the stream" with the safe and known, "the humming street, and the child with its toy ... the priest, the bell and the holy well." "A Summer Night" embodies the same opposition. Unable to give himself entirely to one type of existence or the other, the poet speaks of being "never by passion quite possessed and never quite benumbed by the world's sway." The conflict appears still again in the opposition between the effortless spontaneous existence on the one hand and the life of strenuous moral effort on the other. But the most interesting variation of the dichotomy is the opposition between the conscious and the unconscious self. Such poems as "Lines Written in Butler's Sermons," "The Buried Life," and "Self-Deception" deal with a conflict between the real self, represented as deeply hidden and for the most part unconscious, and the unreal self of everyday existence. Arnold was haunted by the difficulty of knowing the real or buried self and speaks often of the "craving" for "a distinct seeing of [one's] own way as far as [one's] own nature is concerned."[7]

For the conflict that manifested itself in these varying guises Arnold was able to find only temporary resolutions. Each of the opposing sets of claims offered too much for Arnold to be able to consider resolving the conflict by abandoning one set of claims in favor of the other. He could not sacrifice the intellect to the feelings, like some of the romantics, but neither could he sacrifice the feelings to the intellect, for that would be to make the mistake Arnold thought Clough was making, to intellectualize his poetry and cut it off from the true sources of imaginative power.[8] Yet while he could not sacrifice one set of claims in order to do justice to the other, neither could he for long reconcile the opposition or bring the conflicting values into harmony. One could not live both the spontaneous life and the life of moral effort; one could not give free play to the imagination and at the same time do justice to the obligations of the practical world;

one could not bring to full development at the same time both the hidden and the open, the unconscious and the conscious self.

Conflicts of this sort belong to some extent to the conditions of life itself; no one is entirely free from them. Yet undoubtedly some conditions of society generate personal conflicts of this kind more commonly than do others, and in a given society there is much variation between individuals in the degree to which they master or are mastered by such opposing goals. The cleavage in Arnold was sufficiently marked so that we cannot dismiss it by regarding it as merely a normal response to human conditions; further explanation is needed.

In his lines on the ebbing of the sea of faith in "Dover Beach," and in the "Stanzas from the Grande Chartreuse," where he writes of the predicament of modern man "wandering between two worlds, one dead, the other powerless to be born," Arnold himself offers an explanation. Emotionally, he says, man needs the warmth and security associated with a system of belief which in the nineteenth century has become untenable. The cleavage between feeling and intellect, Arnold would seem to be saying, has its source in the fact that our feelings are attuned to the value system of religion or myth which the modern intellect must reject. But one thinks of men like Samuel Butler or William Morris, to mention only two, who were able to discard older forms of faith without experiencing anything like the cleavage that is so marked in Arnold. We know too much about man's adaptability to changes in the intellectual climate to be wholly satisfied with an explanation that confines itself entirely to the consequences of the nineteenth-century disintegration of religion or of myth. While the explanation Arnold offers undoubtedly contains a measure of truth, we can hardly feel that it takes us more than part way toward understanding of the problem.

Should one regard the conflict in Arnold, then, as having

its source in the unconscious—in some form of psychic repression? Often one feels that Arnold's carefully guarded lucidity may be serving as a defense against anarchic drives imperfectly repressed. In their verbal lashing against sexual looseness, parts of Arnold's later essays are almost identical in tone with certain passages in Ruskin, and it is safe to assume that this kind of hysterical Puritanism had its source in psychic repression in Arnold as it undoubtedly did in Ruskin. Yet while there is unquestionably a measure of validity in attributing the conflict in Arnold to psychological repression, the explanation does not impress one, any more than the previous explanation, as being in itself sufficient. The conflict in Arnold, one feels, had a social character which neither the explanation in terms of the breakdown of faith nor the explanation in terms of personal psychology takes into account. To make clear the social character of the conflict, it will be necessary to consider in some detail Arnold's relationship to the society of his day.

As one turns to consider Arnold's adjustment to Victorian society, one discovers that in a number of ways he was closer in spirit to the middle class than he knew. Arnold never tired of ridiculing the Philistinism of the middle class. He was forever talking about the dismal lives these people led, and deriding them for their worship of coal, population, and money, to say nothing of their sense of the importance of a man's right to marry his deceased wife's sister. Yet while Arnold consciously satirized the middle class, he unconsciously manifested some of the essentials of the middle-class spirit. We see this best, perhaps, in the philosophy of history which Arnold developed to serve as framework for his critical theory. For it was to a philosophy of history, rather than to metaphysics, that Arnold looked for the "intellectual deliverance," which comes, as he said, "when we have acquired that harmonious acquiescence of mind which we feel in contemplating a grand spectacle that is intelligible to us; when we have lost that impatient irritation of mind which we feel in presence of an immense, moving, confused spectacle which, while it perpetually excites our curiosity, perpetually baffles our comprehension."[9] The function of the critic, Arnold believed, was so to understand history as to make clear the meaning of the present. "Formerly," one of his notebook quotations reads, *"la critique n'était que l'art de tout discuter; now, la critique est l'art de tout comprendre et de tout expliquer par l'histoire."*[10] When we examine the philosophy of history which supports Arnold's criticism, we have no difficulty in seeing his affinities with the expanding, confident middle class of his time—affinities that are otherwise concealed from us by the tone of detached irony with which Arnold speaks of the Philistine temper.

One is struck first by the positive or empirical habit of mind that Arnold brings to the study of all phases of human experience. Arnold praised Goethe for the way he took nothing on faith, but in examining man's institutions invariably appealed to experience and asked how well each institution served the actual, present needs of men. Arnold himself possessed the detachment from the dominion of the past for which he praised Goethe; it constitutes a main feature of the modernity of his mind. He had the empiricist's scorn for those who cannot live without fairy tales, those who see one superstition discredited only to attach themselves to another, and believe that "because there are no fairies, therefore there must be gnomes." "There are neither fairies nor gnomes, but nature and the course of nature."[11] He believed literary studies would continue to satisfy certain of the practical needs of men, and was therefore able to champion the humanities without exhibiting the anxiety about their fate that so many other nineteenth- and twentieth-century advocates have displayed. Literary studies, he said, serve the "real needs of men" in ways that no other studies can match; "the instinct for self-preservation in humanity," therefore, will preserve them. When he spoke of the aristocracy, or the state, or Protestantism, the test for Arnold was invariably an empirical one; how well, he always asks, does a particular institution meet man's needs today? Now this empirical attitude was in fact a distinguishing feature of the middle class of the Reform Bill period, for it was the historic role of this class to subject traditional institutions to the test of experience, to dissolve institutions which failed to meet the test, and to establish new institutions adapted to man's practical contemporary needs. Arnold had small respect for Jeremy Bentham, but he shared one of the best features of Bentham's mind.

Related to Arnold's empiricism is his flexibility—his freedom from rigidity in thinking and from dogmatism, his relativity in point of view. While advancing one view of a given subject, Arnold has a way of taking into account a quite different view which the first might be expected, for most thinkers at any rate, to exclude. Aware as he was of the meanness of acquisitive goals, he readily admitted, for example, that the fortune-hunting of the middle class might well be performing a useful role.[12] Aware as he was of the value of an extension of the suffrage and of increased political liberty, he at the same time asserted that those who devoted their lives to securing these ends were being sacrificed to "machinery."[13] Arnold's flexibility led him constantly to ask not what a given institution was in itself, but what its actual role was at a particular time, in a particular context. When the question was raised as to whether the Italians were justified in their struggle to achieve national independence, Arnold asserted that "everything depends on the merits of the particular case in which the principle of nationality is invoked. When this principle is invoked on behalf of Italy, its invokers are to be met, not by absurdly denouncing the principle altogether, but by examining whether they invoke it reasonably" in this particular instance.[14] An institution that had served well in one time and place, Arnold insisted, might have nothing but harmful effects in another time and place. The aristocracy, for example, had served a useful purpose in the medieval period when great landed properties provided a shelter from anarchy for the pursuits of civilization, but the lords "in broadcloth and tweed" of the mid-nineteenth century were an anachronism.[15] In the Napoleonic period the aristocracy had served a useful purpose because of its capacity for action in defense of the established fact, but in a time like the present that called for ideas the aristocracy had little to offer.[16]

Similarly, while agreeing that the powerful state in the seventeenth century had been a dangerous development, Arnold at the same time believed that those who warned against the powerful state in the nineteenth century were misguided.[17] "I will not deny that to give a more prominent part to the State would be a considerable change in this country, that maxims once very sound, and habits once very salutary, may be appealed to against it. The sole question is, whether those maxims and habits are sound and salutary at this moment."[18] Readers of Arnold today are so conscious of the dangers of the powerful state that they are inclined to take him to task for his advocacy of a strong central government; but to do this is to judge conditions in Arnold's day by conditions in our own, and in so doing to show oneself deficient in the very quality of flexibility which enabled Arnold to distinguish between conditions in the seventeenth century and those in the nineteenth. Arnold did not propose an increase in state power in the abstract—his flexibility of mind would not permit him to propose anything in the abstract; he proposed an increase in state power in the limited context of mid-Victorian England.

Arnold's flexibility constitutes a further link with the middle class. To be sure, he accused members of the middle class of want of flexibility. Often, as in his discussion of state power, he insisted on the need for relativity of judgment precisely because he saw that the middle class was unable to approach the matter except through an appeal to rigid precept and abstract doctrine. But relativity of mind, one should remember, is itself a relative thing. A class striving for power may manifest a high degree of flexibility in judgment, but may nevertheless come soon to rely on absolutes when called upon to defend an achieved status from the threat of further change. In 1832, when the aristocracy continued to exhibit-the rigid thinking to which it had long been habituated, members of the middle class, engaged in the process of freeing themselves from traditional formulae, were ready to adopt untried points of view, and displayed a marked capacity for flexible judgments; but in later decades the same class, put in a position where it was called upon to defend rather than transform institutions, lost to some degree its flexibility in temper. Though Arnold had occasion to take the middle class to task, then, for want of flexibility, it is still true to say that this quality links him, as does his empiricism, with the middle class at its moment of greatest insurgent strength.

A further link with the middle class appears in the emphasis on change, advance, and progress that marks Arnold's speculations concerning the meaning of the historic process. In these speculations Arnold is in search of a law of development. People attribute the alternation between the Liberals and Conservatives, he says, to the capriciousness of the voters: "But it is not so. Instinctively, however slowly, the human spirit struggles toward the light, and the adoptions and rejections of its agents by the multitude are never wholly blind and capricious, but have a meaning."[19] Similarly, in the course of European history Arnold finds not merely a process of action and reaction, but a dialectical advance in which first one side of the human spirit, and then another, is carried to a high level of development. In the ancient world, according to one of Arnold's formulations, the life of the understanding and of the senses was richly developed. During the Middle Ages there was a reaction against the one-sidedness of the pagan ideal; now opposite qualities, man's capacity for conduct and for spiritual experience, were carried to a high point of development. During the Renaissance a return to the pagan ideal brought a further enrichment of the life of the senses and of the understanding. The Reformation, like the transition from the classical to the medieval period before it, brought a "reaction of the moral and spiritual sense against the carnal and pagan sense." Then again in the eighteenth century came a "grand reaction against the rule of the heart and the imagination, the strong return towards the rule of the senses and understanding."[20] In *Culture and Anarchy* Arnold describes this dialectical advance in terms of the struggle between Hebraism and Hellenism. Hellenism was highly developed in the ancient world, Hebraism in the Middle Ages, Hellenism in the Renaissance, and Hebraism in the Reformation. The main spirit of modern times, he adds, is Hellenism; the Hebraism of the Puritan heritage is a current running counter to the main movement of the age.[21]

In all of Arnold's speculations concerning the historical process—speculations which add up to a philosophy of history so impressive in its comprehensiveness and inner consistency that one wonders that students of Arnold have taken little notice of it—one observes that he is seeking for the principle in history of growth, development, progress. He has much to say about classes, for his empirical habit of mind made him regard the class rather than, like Carlyle, the individual, as the instrument of advance. Here he points out ways in which a particular class, often at the sacrifice of other qualities, serves to bring one aspect of the human spirit to the highest point of development it has yet achieved. The aristocracy, he says, has brought to its highest point the power of social life and manners, though at the cost of a deficiency in ideas. The middle class has developed the power of conduct, though at the cost of a deficiency in knowledge, social life and manners, and beauty. Arnold has much to say also about the role of the nation in the dialectical advance. History, he says, is "a series of waves, coming gradually to a head and then breaking. . . . As the successive waves come up, one nation is seen at the top of this wave, then another of the next."[22] In working out this theory Arnold perhaps reflects the influence of Jules Michelet—whom he was reading, one notes, in 1868, the year before *Culture and Anarchy* was published.[23] Herder, Hegel, von Ranke, Condorcet, and Comte, among others, have advanced a somewhat comparable theory. Yet Arnold's view appears to be his own, not borrowed. We see one example of this in the way he associates particular nations with his own formulation of the "powers" of the human spirit. England, he says, has carried furthest the power of conduct, Italy the power of beauty, Germany the power of knowledge, and France the power of social life and manners.[24]

The essential feature of these speculations for present purposes is Arnold's assumption that history must be regarded as a process of dialectical advance in which the past fulfills itself, only to be superseded by a new mode of development which itself will be superseded in its turn. Every institution, he suggests, may carry within itself the principle of its own negation to ensure that sooner or later it will give way to a higher form of development. "Perhaps everything, take it at what point in its existence you will, carries within itself the fatal law of its ulterior development. Perhaps, even of the life of Pindar's time, Pompeii was the inevitable bourne."[25] Or, as he puts it in another passage that not less than the preceding has a Hegelian ring: "Human thought, which made all institutions, inevitably saps them, resting only in that which is absolute and eternal."[26] In placing stress not on permanence but on change, in finding the key to the meaning of history in a process of perpetual advance, Arnold embodies, not the superficial views obviously, but the fundamental outlook of a class whose grand accomplishment was to break up hereditary institutions, to destroy what was fixed and traditional, and to create new forms of social cohesion—the class whose role it was in its most progressive period to be itself the conscious instrument of social advance. Arnold's view of history has little in common with the crude view of progress in which an accumulation of goods is taken as evidence of an increase in human welfare—the view of Macaulay, for example. It is not the Rotarian view of progress. But like the thinking of Macaulay and the Rotary Club, it derives its confidence and its very character from the power and assurance of the middle class.

The link between Arnold and the middle class appears stronger as one examines his comments on the *Zeitgeist* of his age. Conscious as he was of the importance of taking into account the influence of a particular time and place, Arnold made great use of the concept of the *Zeitgeist,* and spoke often of the way each generation establishes its own special character: "The taste and ideas of one generation are not those of the next. This generation in its turn arrives;—first its sharpshooters, its quick-witted, audacious light troops; then the elephantine main body. The imposing array of its predecessor it confidently assails, riddles it with bullets, passes over its body. It goes hard then with many popular reputations, with many authorities once oracular."[27] The first requirement for the critic, in Arnold's view, is to make a correct estimate of his own moment in history; he believed that he himself had been able to do this, that he understood the time-spirit of mid-nineteenth-century England.

He characterized his own time by showing how it differed from the previous period, whose character had been determined by the struggle against Napoleon. The earlier period had been a time for concentration; this was a time for expansion.[28] The earlier period had been a time for action in defense of the established fact; this was a time for ideas and experiment.[29] Of the *Zeitgeist* of the earlier period Burke had been the spokesman; though he exaggerated the virtues of the old society and the dangers of the new, his thinking on the whole had answered the needs of the age. Now, however, in a time calling for expansion, Burke could be of little use.[30] The present period required a free development of the intellect, a capacity for theory and experiment, and willingness to try out new ideas: "Indeed, I am convinced that as

Science, meaning a true knowledge of things as the basis of our operations, becomes, as it does become, more of a power in the world, the weight of the nations and men who have carried the intellectual life farthest will be more and more felt; indeed, I see signs of this already. That England may run well in this race is my deepest desire; and to stimulate her and to make her feel how many clogs she wears, and how much she has to do in order to run it as her genius gives her the power to run, is the object of all I do."[31] His own age, he says again, is a time that calls for performance of "a work of which it is the great glory of the French Revolution . . . passionately to have embraced the idea: the work of making human life, hampered by a past which it has outgrown, natural and rational."[32]

The great task of the age, the task which established the character of the time-spirit, as Arnold put it in another formulation, was to liberate the vital forces of the nation from outworn institutional restraints. A contradiction existed throughout modern Europe, but especially in England, he pointed out, between the "modern spirit"—the spirit of liberty, equality, and "expansion" which had been given its greatest impetus by the French Revolution—and the institutions of great landed property inherited from the Middle Ages. When the contradiction became insupportable, he predicted, the institutions would have to give way, just as earlier "the Venetian and French aristocracies fell because they could not deal with the ideas of modern Europe."[33] It was America's good fortune, Arnold said, that the contradiction between vital forces and institutions did not exist there. The Americans have institutions which suit them,[34] he said, and the American community in consequence "sees its political and social concerns straight, and sees them clear."[35] In contrast he pointed to "the blinking and hushing up system" which in England grows out of the contradiction between the modern spirit and antiquated institutions.[36] The British are "like people whose vision is deranged by their looking through a turbid and distorting atmosphere, or whose movements are warped by the cramping of some unnatural constraint."[37] In an age whose spirit was born of the French Revolution England's institutions perpetuate a "religion of inequality" appropriate to the Middle Ages. "Our very classes make us dim-seeing. In a modern time, we are living with a system of classes so intense, a society of such unnatural complication, that the whole action of our minds is hampered and falsened by it."[38]

In these passages Arnold clearly assumes that it is the inheritance of the aristocracy that places restraints upon the free development of the modern spirit, and while he associates the work of liberation not so much with a class as with a spirit—the modern spirit—yet he makes it clear that the function he ascribes to the modern spirit, that of breaking down the restrictions of the past and making room for a great movement of "expansion," was precisely the function of the middle class in nineteenth-century England, the middle class, especially, of the Reform Bill and anti-Corn Law period. Once again, then, we see an identity between Arnold's view and that of the progressive class of his time.

In his estimate of the potentialities of the present, furthermore, Arnold had all the optimism of the class that, having recently achieved power, was developing new manufactures, opening new markets, increasing the flow of goods, and in short leading the world in the establishment of a new and fabulously productive economy. Arnold's optimism was not naïve, any more than his conception of historical development was naïve. But a prophecy such as he makes in *A French Eton,* that the "children of the future" will at a distant time in their turn be "mounting some new step in the arduous ladder whereby man climbs towards his perfection," could be made only in a supremely confident age.[39] Frederic Harrison rightly said that Arnold was "constantly talking Comte without knowing it."[40]

Arnold's account of the "perfected society" toward which

the dialectical movement of history is aimed remains as one of the noblest embodiments of the reaches of the human spirit in the nineteenth century. We are striving, he says, for a civilization which will enable all men to realize their "true aspirations and powers."[41] A civilization that develops only certain of the characteristic "powers" of the human spirit—the power of intellect and knowledge, of social life and manners, of conduct, and of beauty—is necessarily incomplete.[42] The "perfected civilization" will develop the four powers harmoniously. It will be a civilization, too, in which the opportunity to live creatively will be extended to all; for Arnold regarded it as "undeniable that the exercise of a creative power, that a free creative activity, is the highest function of man; it is proved to be so by man's finding in it his true happiness."[43] We shall achieve "progress towards man's best perfection—the adorning and ennobling of his spirit,"[44] then, in so far as people are enabled to cultivate the other specifically human powers, and at the same time to discover and exercise their own creativity. The perfected society will resemble "the epochs of Aeschylus and Shakespeare"—it is there that we must look for "the promised land, towards which criticism can only beckon."[45]

Arnold's account of the perfected society has an integrity and persuasiveness that utopias generally lack. Delightful as is William Morris's *News from Nowhere,* for example, one cannot help feeling that the idyllic life he describes is a rather empty one. Unlike Morris—and unlike Carlyle and Ruskin also—Arnold looks forward not to a simplification of existence but to a civilization of heightened maturity and complexity. There is no question that here Arnold transcends the limits of the middle class and speaks in a sense as the heir to all the ages, for this is a vision that draws upon the free play of the mind in the ancient world as well as the expansion of knowledge in more recent centuries, the devotion to beauty of the Greeks and the Renaissance as well as the ethical concern of the Puritan middle class. Arnold presents a large, luminous, and imaginative view of the possibilities of human development. He does so with feeling and at the same time with the hardheadedness toward which his critical and positive intelligence disposed him. He proposes a break with the past and at the same time resolves to capitalize on the past's inheritance. Yet it is not fanciful to say, paradoxically, that in transcending the limitations of his age Arnold gave expression to the best the age had in it to produce, for he belonged to one of those periods of creative advance when the leading class becomes a representative not of itself alone but of the cause of humanity, combining the resolve to salvage the best in the past with the resolve to move boldly toward the future.

Arnold is considerably more than the shrewdest critic of the middle class, then; he is also a spokesman for the best characteristics of that class at its moment of great achievement and of confident power. But there is still another way in which he is allied to the middle class of his time. To understand this still deeper affinity we must call to mind the terror as well as the confidence of the age. To do so is not easy, for the fallacy that the Victorian age was serene continues to obscure for us the sense of peril, the threat of catastrophe, of which those who lived then were acutely aware.

When the Reform Bill was passed, as we have seen, the temper of the people was sufficiently rebellious so that many, of whom Carlyle was one, believed that England was on the verge of the kind of social upheaval that had taken place in France forty years earlier. Throughout the period from 1832 to 1848 this fear remained, and with good reason. Disenchantment with the Reform Bill on the part of the working class was almost immediate, and the great protest against the established order which had gone into the Reform agitation soon manifested itself in struggle against the Poor Law and a little later in Chartism. It is true that many of those who suffered most from the evils of the new order were too demoralized, or spiritually diseased, to offer any serious threat to the status quo. Often they were so demoralized as to rebel against legislation intended to benefit them. One hears of factory workers resisting a proposal of their employers to install flues to carry off dust, out of fear that if conditions of work improved the supply of labor would rise and wages go down.[46] In Elizabeth Gaskell's *Mary Barton,* the workers themselves are represented as protesting against legislation limiting child labor: "What a sore trial it is," says Mrs. Davenport, "this law o' theirs, keeping childer fra' factory work, whether they be weakly or strong."[47] Yet despite instances of demoralization like these, a sufficient number of working people displayed clarity and vigor in their efforts to secure changes in the established order to justify the apprehension that continued throughout these decades. In 1839, 1842, and 1848, waves of Chartist agitation, following periods of depression and unemployment, brought the country close to the point of revolution. These were times of monster meetings, attended by crowds up to two hundred thousand.[48] Plans were made for a general strike. Feargus O'Connor was advocating armed rebellion.[49] Many who attended the Chartist meetings wore tricolor cockades and caps of liberty. One of the Chartist leaders described himself as the British Marat. The delegates to the Chartist convention in London argued in 1839 that the convention was the only true parliament, that the "rotten" parliament should be disregarded. Men were in arms throughout the country ready to support their claims.[50]

For a period of about twenty-five years, it is true, from 1850 to 1875, a measure of stabilization was achieved. This is the period G. D. H. Cole describes as the Golden Age of British Capitalism.[51] The working class now to some degree forgot its revolutionary aims. "Trade revived, and Socialism decayed," as Bertrand Russell says.[52] Yet even during this period there were periodic depressions, those of 1857 and 1866 being the most serious. Maccoby believes that Disraeli would not have obtained passage of the second Reform Bill if the temper of the populace had not been dangerously restive.⁵³ And as a matter of fact it was precisely at this time, at the very mid-point of the Golden Age, that Matthew Arnold became most panicky about the threat of anarchy. After 1875 came the economic collapse which initiated the prolonged trade depression of the eighties, and with the founding of modern socialist parties the agitation for a change in the established order became once again almost as conscious and militant as in the days of Chartism.

The two most important stabilizing forces of the first half of the nineteenth century, the humanitarian movement and the religious revival, should properly be thought of as indications not of the stability but of the instability of the social order, for it was in part at least the sense of acute social unrest that brought these two movements into being. Lord Shaftesbury, the chief humanitarian leader of the age, avowed explicitly that the role of the humanitarian movement was to stave off the demand for a radical change in the existing order. He wrote in his diary in 1842 that the workers were subordinating all other considerations to the Charter, and added that if the government had accepted the factory reforms he proposed, there would have been no Charter.⁵⁴ In *Mary Barton,* described by Thomas Seccombe as "the starting-point and rallying-cry of a new generation of humanitarians,"⁵⁵ Elizabeth Gaskell appeals for alleviation of the plight of the workers because their terrible destitution, if not diminished, must lead to violence.⁵⁶ "At present," she says, the workers of Manchester "seem to me to be left in a state wherein lamentation and tears are thrown aside as useless, but in which the lips are compressed for curses, and the hands clenched and ready to smite."⁵⁷ At least one aim of the humanitarian movement was to withhold the clenched fist from its intended blow.

The religious revival, similarly, had everywhere as one of its functions, and often as one of its avowed aims, a blunting of the revolutionary energies of the people. Halévy believes that it was primarily the Evangelical movement of the first half of the nineteenth century that saved England from revolution.[58] For the Evangelicals, like members of other religious sects, taught—to quote from Lady Eastlake's review of *Jane Eyre*—that "murmuring against the comforts of the rich and against the privations of the poor" amounted to "a murmuring against God's appointment."[59] It was because the followers of Wesley used religion in defense of what many regarded as an evil system that Cobbett spoke of them as the "nasty, canting, dirty, lousy Methodists."[60] Even Charles Kingsley, though he had enough enthusiasm for the Charter to appall a man like Froude,[61] told the Chartists that religion, rather than the Charter, was what they needed. "You think the Charter would make you free—," he wrote, and the words were posted on placards throughout London on April 11, 1848; "would to God it would. The Charter is not bad, if the men who use it are not bad! But will the Charter make you free? Will it free you from the slavery of ten-pound bribes? Slavery to gin and beer? Slavery to every spouter who flatters your self-conceit, and stirs up bitterness and headlong rage in you? That, I guess, is real slavery: to be a slave to one's own stomach, one's own pocket, one's own temper. Will the Charter cure that? Friends, you want more than Acts of Parliament can give."[62] In *Politics for the People*, the Christian Socialist periodical edited by F. D. Maurice, Kingsley amplified his thesis that religious conviction would better answer the needs of the workers than achievement of their Chartist aims: "I think you have fallen into the same mistake as the rich of whom you complain—," he says, "the very mistake which has been our curse and our nightmare—I mean the mistake of fancying that legislative reform is social reform, or that men's hearts can be changed by Act of Parliament. If anyone can tell me of a country where a charter has made the rogues honest, or the idle industrious, I shall alter my opinion of the Charter, but not till then."[63] While it is true, then, that the humanitarian movement and the religious revival were stabilizing forces, these movements may at the same time be viewed as evidence of the unrest of the time, for it was the threat of social upheaval, in part, that motivated the leaders of both movements. A further indication of the unrest of the times is the fact that the manufacturing class felt it necessary to direct toward the workers a great propaganda intended to persuade them that they must solve their problems within the system, not outside it. Lord Brougham's "steam intellect society," though it had little effect in the thirties and forties, exercised considerable influence thereafter.[64] The aim of this organization was to persuade the working man that he "had a commodity to sell like anyone else—his labor—and his only way to prosperity was to raise its price. This he could do individually by improving his skill as a craftsman, saving his money, working hard, and living temperately. By this means he would himself become an article of rare value and his price would rise: his fellows, by doing the same, would increase the general wealth and keep goods in rapid circulation. Universal abundance would result, except, of course, for the idle, turbulent, or debauched. Friendly societies were prudent and laudable institutions; Trade Unions, by calling strikes and violently stopping the wheels of industry, merely spread desolation and despair."[65]

Despite the humanitarian movement, the religious revival, and the efforts of employers to indoctrinate the workers concerning the benefits of the system, the temper of the masses remained uncertain throughout most of the century. It might perhaps be argued that England in the nineteenth century escaped the violent social disturbances that took place in France mainly because of special circumstances which brought it about that the working class enlisted itself repeatedly in struggles on behalf of the middle class, though the aim of working-class leaders was to fight not with the middle class but against it. In the forties, for example, as earlier in the Reform Bill period, the manufacturers succeeded in recruiting large sections of the working class in a struggle to increase middle-class power. It is significant that the Anti-Corn-Law League was formed in 1838, the year when Chartism first became a dangerous threat. Elie Halévy believes that the free trade agitation of the Anti-Corn-Law League was thought up by the employers and their representatives in parliament in order to provide a substitute for Chartist agitation—to provide an issue that could unite the workers with the employers against the landed class.[66] The free traders urged workingmen not to waste their time agitating for reduction of the working day, or for the six points of the Charter, or for increased wages, but instead to join their masters in a campaign to remove the duty on grain. In appealing to the workers in this way, the middle-class leaders were far from being demagogues; they were sincere men— idealists, as a matter of fact. They were justified, too, in their claim that in the long run repeal of the corn laws should benefit the workers as well as the manufacturers; for this was a time when, as John Morley says, "the class-interest of the manufacturers and merchants happened to fall in with the good of the rest of the community; while the class-interest against which they were going up to battle, was an uncompensated burden on the whole commonwealth."[67] The immediate interests of the manufacturers "widened into the consciousness of a commanding national interest."[68] This was one of those situations in which "a powerful class," in the words of Bertrand Russell, "could advocate its own interests while furthering the general good. Such situations are apt to call forth as leaders men of broad and humane outlook, in whom the element of self-interest is concealed by public spirit."[69] "The hard-headed man of business," Morley says, "gradually felt himself touched with the generous glow of the patriot and the deliverer."[70] For Cobden the free-trade agitation was not merely a commercial movement; it was a moral, even a religious, mission.[71] He spoke of free trade as "the means—and I believe the only human means—of effecting universal and permanent peace."[72]

It is not surprising that the manufacturers succeeded in

diverting a part of the working class into such a crusade as this. Yet they gained working-class support only with difficulty. The Chartists at first insisted that the agitation was a cheat put upon the workers by "cunning and rapacious" employers.[73] Feargus O'Connor and the Chartist revolutionaries led by Bronterre O'Brien insisted that the working class had little to gain from free trade and should stick to its class objectives.[74] Toward the end of 1838 both agitations were carried on at the same time, the Chartists and free traders holding rival meetings.[75] But soon a sizable portion of the working class was enlisted in the anti-Corn-Law agitation; the intensity and violence with which the free-trade campaign was henceforth carried on is evidence that the revolutionary energies of the working class were finding expression in this movement just as they had previously found expression in the agitation for reform. The free traders were now described in the Tory press as swindlers and socialists. They were denied meeting places, forced to speak in the market places, then arrested for obstructing the thoroughfare. They had to form bodyguards for protection against mobs incited by the landlords.[76] Meanwhile they circulated mass petitions, organized delegated meetings, passed resolutions, gathered statistics, and set up their own press.[77] The mass pressures that had built the Chartist movement, in other words, were successfully diverted into a middle-class movement.

In foreign as well as domestic policy the working class repeatedly found itself allied with the middle class instead of in opposition to it. The consequent loss of autonomy and militancy on the part of the working class goes far to explain why the threat of an insurgent working-class advance failed to materialize. In the long struggle with Russia, in which England fought the Crimean War in the fifties and came close to fighting another war in the seventies, the radical movement was invariably divided "into a non-interventionist wing . . . and an extreme democratic wing anxious for intervention in support of liberty against 'tyranny and oppression.' "[78] "In theory," says Maccoby, "all wings of Radicalism throughout the period would have accepted as the axiom of their foreign policy hostility to wars of pure aggrandizement by the British Government,"[79] but in each particular instance it was hard to tell whether the contest with Russia should be viewed as a struggle for aggrandizement by Great Britain or as a defense of freedom against Czarist tyranny. The theoretical difficulty here was comparable, needless to say, with the difficulty faced by left-wing movements in Western European countries and in America in formulating a policy toward Hitler before the Second World War. Should preparation for a struggle against Hitler be viewed as power politics by the governments of the West or as a crusade for democracy against fascism? In 1877 a left-wing Trafalgar Square meeting called to protest against preparations for an imperialist war against Russia clashed with another left-wing meeting called to demand that England take action against the tyranny and aggression of the Czar.[80] In precisely the same way did left-wing groups demanding intervention clash with left-wing groups demanding nonintervention in countries threatened by fascism in the nineteen-thirties. The weakening of the radical movement by this conflict over foreign policy was of course incalculable. Yet in spite of the way the working class spent its strength in fighting middle-class battles and in a self-defeating conflict over foreign policy, it nevertheless retained sufficient strength throughout most of the period to justify the apprehension that was so widely felt concerning the stability of the existing order.

One reason why historians of nineteenth-century England place insufficient stress on the social unrest of the period is that many of the sources historians use are contemporary accounts written by men who purposely minimized the strength of radical pressures. According to Maccoby, it was generally mass pressure that brought about the political reforms of the period, but everything was done, he says, to give the credit to the enlightened statesmanship of the leaders of government. "When 'pressure from without' had become highly inconvenient and even positively dangerous," he says, "a modicum of sedative legislative compromise was prepared in which all 'the settled institutions of the country' were most carefully safeguarded." Further "safeguarding" would then be insisted upon by the ultra-conservative House of Lords. " 'Public opinion,' finally, in the shape of *The Times* newspaper and the like, hastened to congratulate an often dubious, jeering, or actively hostile populace on living in the liberal and progressive era which permitted 'great changes' to take place peacefully almost every year."[81]

Matthew Arnold was no less responsive to the perils of the age than he was to its promise. He feared just as strongly as he welcomed what he took to be the dominant tendency of the age—continuation and fulfillment of the work of the French Revolution. To sweep away the inheritance of feudalism, to put an end to immense privilege, to widen the scope of liberty, democracy, equality—this, he believed, was the business of the hour, the work of the "modern spirit." But his attitude toward the modern spirit was at all times an ambivalent one. On the one hand the changes wrought by the modern spirit were freeing men from the senseless bondage of the past and creating the necessary pre-conditions for a high state of civilization. On the other hand the modern spirit threatened to create a leveled and vulgarized society; it threatened, worse still, to release the wrecking impulses of the mob and so lead to a state of civil disorder "where each thing meets in mere oppugnancy." Arnold looked on the creative potentialities of the modern spirit with hopeful confidence and on its menace with dismay; it was a spirit, to refer to the title of Arnold's famous book, that promised culture and threatened anarchy. Instead of abandoning one of the conflicting responses in favor of the other, or successfully combining them, as he tried to do, in some higher synthesis where the integrity of each might be maintained despite the existence of its opposite, he held the opposing responses in perilous conflict throughout his adult life, and permitted the emotional antagonism to which they gave rise to paralyze a part of his nature.

In the revolutionary year of 1848 Arnold shared the fervor of those who saw about them the promise of a better world. He announced proudly that "the hour of the hereditary peerage and eldest sonship and immense properties has, I am convinced . . . struck."[82] Yet in the same year he wrote to Clough: "For my part I cannot *understand* this violent praise of the people; I praise a fagot whereof the several twigs are nought, but a *people?*"[83] When there were indications that the Revolution of 1848 might cross the Channel, he wrote to his sister "K" that the state of the masses in England was such that "brutal plundering and destroying" were all that could be expected of them.[84]

In 1856 Arnold told K that it was his belief that "the English aristocratic system, splendid fruits as it has undoubtedly borne, must go," but quickly he set down the opposing consideration: "It does not rejoice me to think this, because what a middle class and people we have in England! of whom Saint-Simon says truly: '*Sur tous les chantiers de l'Angleterre il n'existe pas une seule grande idée.*' "[85] When he began his prose criticism with *England and the Italian Question* (1859) and *Popular Education in France* (1861) (the preface to which was later published in *Mixed Essays* under the title "Democracy"), Arnold again showed himself divided between the two opposing considerations. Now is the time, he says, for "the ideas of religious, political, and social freedom, which are commonly called the ideas of 1789"; the time has come for that "irresistible force, which is gradually making its way everywhere, removing old conditions and imposing new, altering long-fixed habits, undermining venerable institutions, even modifying national character: *the modern spirit.*"[86] Yet is there not great danger, he adds, that the modern spirit will bring into being a standardized, Philistinized, "Americanized" society—a society characterized by the vulgarity and bathos that must result when the multitude comes to power with no "adequate ideal" to elevate and guide it?

As he continues with the main body of his critical work in the sixties, the same ambivalence appears. In "The Function of Criticism at the Present Time" (1864) he describes the French Revolution as "the greatest, most animating event in history";[87] the present, he adds, is the time to put the revolutionary ideas of democracy and equality into practice. But in saying this he hardly conceals his panic lest the attempt to give "immediate and practical application" to the new ideas should move too fast and get out of control.[88] In the essay on Joubert, published in the same year (1864), he returns to the warning that to give premature application to ideas of democracy and equality is dangerous no matter how sound these ideas may be in theory.[89]

Culture and Anarchy (1869) gives further evidence of the same conflict. On the one hand the book is a magnificent affirmation of the modern spirit. "What is alone and always sacred and binding for man is the making progress towards his best perfection."[90] The familiar tags of *Culture and Anarchy*—making "reason and the will of God prevail," "the study of perfection," the need for "a current of fresh and true ideas"—remind us of the note of affirmation in the book. We are moving, Arnold says, toward "the general harmonious expansion of those gifts of thought and feeling, which make the peculiar dignity, wealth, and happiness of human nature."[91] We are approaching, it may be, one of "the flowering times for literature and art and all the creative power of genius, when there is a *national* glow of life and thought, when the whole society is in the fullest measure permeated by thought, sensible to beauty, intelligent and alive."[92] But in the midst of these trumpet notes heralding the new age we hear the cry of alarm. Again Arnold shudders at the vista of "Americanized" hordes making up a society where "the concerns of life [are] limited to these two: the concern for making money, and the concern for saving souls."[93] He is appalled at the menace of "Jacobinism."[94] In tones reminiscent of Carlyle's hysteria he expresses his contempt for the officer who was too timid to shoot down Hyde Park rioters at the time of the second Reform Bill.[95] "For my part, I do not object, wherever I see disorder, to see coercion applied to it," he says. So oddly does Arnold at times unite the language of liberalism with advocacy of force, as to remind the reader of William Morris's parody of the liberal newspaper which, "after a preamble in which it declared its undeviating sympathy with the cause of labor, proceeded to point out that in times of revolutionary disturbance it behooved the Government to be just but firm, and that by far the most merciful way of dealing with the poor madmen who were attacking the foundations of society (which had made them mad and poor) was to shoot them at once."[96] Arnold's fear of anarchy carries him to the point where he lays down the proposition that "the framework and exterior order of the State, whosoever may administer the State, is sacred"[97]—a proposition dictators would find congenial.

Ten years later, in "Equality," the antithetical attitudes toward the modern spirit manifest themselves again. The hope for the future rests upon an extension of equality, he says. "Our shortcomings in civilization are due to our inequality. . . . The great inequality of classes and property, which came to us from the Middle Age and which we maintain because we have the religion of inequality . . . has the natural and necessary effect, under present circumstances, of materializing our upper class, vulgarizing our middle class, and brutalizing our lower class. And this is to fail in civilization."[98] Then Arnold thinks of the dangers of the modern spirit and is swept into the opposing current of thought. In America, he tells us once again, "we see the disadvantages of having social equality before there has been any . . . high standard of social life and manners formed."[99] Let us conserve what exists, he concludes, rather than risk the perils of change. "Our present social organization will and must endure until our middle class is provided with some better ideal of life than it has now."[100]

In the last decade of his life it is the same. In "A Word More about America" (1885) he praises America because the modern spirit has here made greater headway than in England. America's democratic institutions are better suited to the needs of the people than are England's; England's failure to put democratic ideas into practice is stultifying the national life.[101] Yet in these very years Arnold's fear of democracy is so great that in "Numbers" (1884) he sets down the Tory doctrine that majorities are always and necessarily unsound.[102] Again he warns that "monster processions and monster meetings in the public streets and parks are the letting out of anarchy, and . . . our weak dealing with them is deplorable."[103] Again he voices his fear of Jacobinism with its "temper of hatred and . . . aim of destruction."[104]

To maintain over a long period of years conflicting attitudes of this nature puts a severe strain upon the personality, and it may be that toward the end of his life Arnold was moving toward a simplified Tory position. He died in 1888—in a crucial period of social change. One would like to know how his thinking would have developed had he lived into the nineties. Near the end of his life Arnold developed the conservative doctrine of the "saving remnant," and he defended Bismarck against the criticism of "advanced liberals" like John Morley, who "are always apt to think that a condition of things where the people cannot hold whatever meetings and processions they like, and wherever they like, is an unnatural condition and likely to dissolve."[105] Though ready to propose so bold a measure as expropriation of the English landlords in Ireland,[106] he dismisses as "madness" the proposal that Ireland be given her own parliament.[107] His comments on the Zulu War of 1879 have something of Kipling's tone. Writing of the defeat of British troops at Isandhlwana on January 22 of that year he conjectures that good may come out of it because it will lead to a more thorough subjugation of the Zulus "and to a more speedy extension of the Englishry as far as the climate will let them extend—that is, about up to the Tropic of Capricorn. And unattractive as the raw Englishry is, it is good stuff, and, always supposing it not to deteriorate but to improve, its spread is the spread of civilization."[108] Arnold's liberal, progressive, or democratic side is in abeyance here. To get the measure of his conservatism one only needs to set beside this comment on the Zulu War what John Morley was saying at the same time. Morley refers to remarks similar to the one Arnold has just made concerning England's "civilizing power": "When I come across such phrases in a blue-book," he says, "I shudder; they always precede a massacre."[109] "Consider the rank hypocrisy of it all," he continues. "At the very moment that we are pharisaically contemplating England as a trustee of special appointment by the heavenly powers in behalf of the more backward races of the earth, we are massacring them by thousands, we are burning their kraals and carrying off their herds, we are breaking up first one and then another of their rudimentary systems of society, we are preparing the reign and authority of a set of men whose only notion of improvement . . . is to improve the unfortunate wards and clients of ours off the face of the earth."[110] If these policies continue, he concludes, "the old realm which was once the home of justice and freedom" will "be transformed into a Pirate-Empire, with the Cross hypocritically chalked upon its black flag."[111] As an indication of the Toryism of Arnold's position one might also contrast William Morris's view of what the "speedy extension of the Englishry" actually entails: "When the civilized world-market coveted a country not yet in its clutches," Morris has Hammond say in a retrospective comment on the nineteenth century in *News from Nowhere,* "some transparent pretext was found,—the suppression of a slavery different from and not as cruel as that of commerce; the pushing of a religion no longer believed in by its promoters; the 'rescue' of some desperado or homicidal madman whose misdeeds had got him into trouble among the natives of the 'barbarous' country,—any stick, in short, which would beat the dog at all. Then some bold, unprincipled, ignorant adventurer was found (no difficult task in the days of competition), and he was bribed to 'create a market' by breaking up whatever traditional society there might be in the doomed country, and by destroying whatever leisure or pleasure he found there. He forced wares upon the natives which they did not want, and took their natural products in 'exchange,' as this form of robbery was called, and thereby he 'created new wants,' to supply which (that is, to be allowed to live by their new masters) the hapless, helpless people had to sell themselves into the slavery of hopeless toil so that they might have something wherewith to purchase the nullities of 'civilization.' "[112]

There is no question that Arnold's conflicting attitudes toward the modern spirit remained until his death, no matter what one may think about his possible approach to a more purely conservative position in the last years. In these conflicting attitudes Arnold embodied the very uncertainty concerning democratic trends that characterized the middle class of his time. There had now developed what Morris calls the "covert alliance between the powerful middle classes who were the children of commerce and their old masters the aristocracy; an unconscious understanding between them rather, in the midst of their contest, that certain matters were to be respected even by the advanced party."[113] Yet the middle class still felt itself curbed by the continuing political and economic power, not to speak of the moral ascendency, of the class of prescriptive privilege and inherited wealth. To a certain degree, in consequence, the middle class still identified itself with the forces of expansion and liberation which stemmed from the French Revolution—a revolution whose role, after all, on the European scene generally, was to bring the middle class to power. At the same time the middle class was immediately confronted with an insurgent working class only too anxious to use revolutionary ideas in its own interest. The very men who responded warmly to the promise of the modern spirit when they conceived themselves as in revolt against aristocratic privilege, were dismayed at the leveling and apparently destructive potentialities of the modern spirit when faced with a working class only too likely to employ the new ideas in a struggle for an egalitarian society. The characteristic attitude of the middle class toward the modern spirit was therefore precisely the ambivalent attitude that Arnold displayed.

In view of Arnold's caustic criticism of the middle class, some readers may hesitate to accept the view that his deepest attitudes were identical with those of the middle class. Yet we know that one cannot disassociate a man from a particular set of attitudes, or attachments, or ideas merely because he disclaims them; if he disclaims them with emotion, in fact, it may be that they have a significant place in his personality. At any rate, once we have discovered that Arnold shared at once the characteristic confidence and the characteristic fear of the middle class, we recall that despite his attack on Philistines he gave us considerable warrant for regarding him as having an especially close relationship to this class. His aim in the writings on education, he was in the habit of saying, was to create a demand for better schools not for people in general—but better schools, specifically, for the middle class. He always gave it as his belief that in the foreseeable future not the aristocracy, not the working class, but the middle class would shape the destiny of England. And then one recalls the remark of William Morris, a shrewd judge of men, that "Matthew Arnold was right about the Philistines, being a good bit of that kidney himself."[114]

Is it not because literary historians have failed to see the middle-class conflict at the heart of Arnold's thinking that they have come to such contradictory conclusions about him? George Saintsbury regards him as a flag-waving Jacobin, ready to leap to the barricades; he can't forgive him for advocating a fraternal type of democracy instead of the legalistic, unembarrassing, English variety.[115] Leonard Woolf[116] and Ernest Barker,[117] on the other hand, regard him as an authoritarian whose views have their logical consequence in absolutism. Dover Wilson, however, protests that Woolf and Barker have misread Arnold; they have not given enough attention to the great essays on "Democracy" and "Equality," and they have missed the quality of Arnold's irony.[118] Lionel Trilling concurs in Dover Wilson's opinion and takes pains to defend Arnold against the charge of authoritarianism.[119] But then comes Howard Mumford Jones to tell us that Arnold is a believer in "racial snobbery and anti-democratic political action," a "Hamiltonian," a "nineteenth-century Colonel Lindbergh."[120] Some historians, in other words, struck mainly by the democratic character of Arnold's thinking, have thought of him as an advocate of modern, even leveling ideas; others, struck mainly by his fear of the masses, have written him off as a Tory. The truth about Arnold is that he was radical and Tory at the same time, that he maintained a delicate and difficult balance between contradictory attitudes toward the modern spirit; and it is precisely this ambivalence that enables us to understand the essentials of his thought.

The conflict is the more significant because, while Arnold's is the most composed and lucid mind in which it can be studied, it is a conflict many of the great authors of the period shared. There is no evidence of such a conflict, to be sure, in Macaulay. Like the Babbitt of a later day, he could see only the forces of expansion and he equated expansion with the accumulation of material goods; his mind did not probe deep enough to make him aware of the divergent significances in modern life of which Arnold was so deeply aware. Nor is there evidence of such a conflict in Newman, who voices only hatred of the ideas whose impetus came from the French Revolution. But Carlyle, Ruskin, Tennyson, and Huxley all exhibit in one form or another contradictory attitudes toward the modern spirit. Carlyle saw the need to sweep aside the old clothes of the past but at the same time he feared the anarchic potentialties of the present. He differed from Arnold, however, in that his fear of the modern spirit was so much stronger than his confidence that where Arnold hesitated between liberal and conservative views Carlyle moved rapidly toward a purely conservative philosophy. Ruskin oscillates between a hopeful and a panicky response to the modern spirit throughout his work, much as Arnold does. In Tennyson we can trace the conflict between opposing responses to the modern spirit from "Locksley Hall" to "Locksley Hall Sixty Years After," and we can trace it, too, in Huxley's essays and lectures, though Huxley, with a mind less sensitive than Arnold's, sometimes takes a view analogous to Macaulay's of what expansion means, and is less aware than Arnold of both the needs and the perils of man's imaginative and spiritual life in modern times. On the whole, the conflict can be studied to greater advantage in Arnold than in any of these other authors of somewhat comparable stature, for his mind was better balanced than Carlyle's or Ruskin's, more forceful and venturesome than Tennyson's, and more sensitive than Huxley's.

The conflict is not merely a nineteenth-century phenomenon, however; it is also perhaps the primary conflict of our own day. One reason why Arnold speaks so directly to the present, it may be, is that both in his poetry and in his prose his singular intelligence and integrity of spirit enabled him to embody better than any other author of his time or of later times the dilemma of modern man.

Conflicts within the personality are of different kinds; some are productive and enriching, others self-defeating. The conflict we are studying in Arnold did not issue in a synthesis through which he could bring the full strength of his personality into productive activity; it left him, instead, emotionally thwarted and intellectually perplexed. Because of this conflict Arnold was unable finally to construct a philosophy that would bring the "harmonious acquiescence of mind" which he tried constantly to believe that he had won—a philosophy that would disclose the order in the "confused spectacle" that "perpetually baffles our comprehension." It was because he failed to develop such a philosophy that his references to the modern world are marked by a tone of weary bafflement, so different from the tone one might expect of a member of "the happiest class of the happiest country in the happiest period of the world."[121] The world is a place of "a thousand discords," he says in "Quiet Work"; he speaks of "man's senseless uproar" and "vain turmoil." We live a distracted existence, he says in "Self-Dependence," and "pine with noting all the fever of some differing soul." He speaks of the "stupefying power" of "all the thousand nothings of the hour."[122] We live "tricked in disguises"; we "pour ourselves in every strife" and become "jaded with the rush and glare of the interminable hours.[123] Nineteenth-century life is a thing of "change, alarm, surprise"; we are like children playing in the surf—no sooner do we recover from one wave than the next knocks us off our feet. We are harassed by "the hopeless tangle of our age."[124] Those who have surrendered to the influences of the time find that "from change to change their being rolls"; "repeated shocks . . . numb their elastic powers"; they suffer from "the sick fatigue, the languid doubt which much to have tried, in much been baffled brings." We are "light half-believers in our casual creeds, who never deeply felt nor clearly willed."[125] The "earthly turmoil" is described in "Thyrsis" as "strange and vain." In "Heine's Grave" Arnold speaks of how "stupidity travels her round of mechanic business." In "Dover Beach"—in the most famous and most terrible of the images—the world is a "darkling plain, swept with confused alarms of struggle and flight, where ignorant armies clash by night."

If Arnold's ambivalent response to the modern world kept him from constructing a philosophy that might have released him from the baffled moods to which these poems testify, it intensified at the same time those personal conflicts which are to be explained in part in terms of other causes. If, like William Morris, he had been able to affirm the democratic side of his nature and to reject or transcend the Hamiltonian, he might have developed, as Morris did, toward what Erich Fromm calls "the only possible, productive solution for the relationship of individualized man with the world: his active solidarity with all men and spontaneous activity, love and work, which unite him again with the world, not by primary ties but as a free and independent individual."[126] Such a relationship with the world Arnold could not achieve. His affirmative response to the modern spirit confirmed and liberated the spontaneous forces of his own nature, while the negative response strengthened the repressive forces; the psychic cleavage, becoming in this fashion the vehicle through which social attitudes expressed themselves, grew more acute than it would otherwise have been. As a result, far from possessing the inner unity and wholeness which alone makes possible productive activity of the kind Fromm describes, Arnold was one of those who anticipated the state of cleavage between thought and feeling that Aldous Huxley defines when he says: "The only satisfactory way of existing in the modern . . . world is to live with two personalities. A Dr. Jekyll that does the metaphysical and scientific thinking, that transacts business in the city, adds up figures, designs machines, and so forth. And a natural, spontaneous Mr. Hyde to do the physical, instinctive living in the intervals of work. The two personalities should lead their unconnected lives apart, without poaching on one another's preserve or enquiring too closely into one another's activities. Only by living discretely and inconsistently can we preserve both the man and the citizen, both the intellectual and the spontaneous animal being, alive within us. The solution may not be very satisfactory; but it is, I believe now (though once I thought differently), the best that, in the modern circumstances, can be devised."[127]

The conflicts embodied in Arnold's poetry are not to be regarded simply as consequences of the conflict in his attitudes toward the modern spirit; they have an integrity of their own. Instinct versus intellect, the "open and liberal" state of youth versus the "morality and character" of age, passion versus conformity, spontaneity versus discipline, the unconscious versus the conscious—these were real issues for Arnold; they were, at least in part, what they seemed. The explanations given earlier of the causes of this sense of cleavage are likewise, up to a point, valid. Arnold was greatly troubled by the fact that the nineteenth century provided no way to satisfy the emotional need for faith or myth and at the same time to maintain one's intellectual integrity. Some form of subconscious or neurotic conflict, too, was almost certainly responsible in part for the perpetuation of the cleavage. These explanations do not tell the whole truth, but they do tell part of it, and they are to be accepted, so far as they go, at face value rather than simply as rationalizations of causes of a different nature. Yet it is still true that expressing themselves through these conflicts were two opposing responses to the modern world. The desire to give free play to the feelings, to spontaneity and instinct, to the principle of expansion was an independent and valid emotional need, but it was an expression at the same time of an affirmative response to the modern spirit, of Arnold's sense that the creative or expansive forces of the modern world were making for a more general fulfillment of human potentialities. The need for discipline, for conformity, for moral strictness and restraint was also an independent and valid need of the personality, but it served as an expression at the same time of the negative response to the modern spirit, of Arnold's sense that the expansive forces were so fraught with anarchic potentialities as to require strict restraint. If it is correct to attribute the sense of cleavage in part to the spiritual dilemma of an age of crumbling faith, and in part to subconscious personal conflicts, it is correct also to attribute it in part to Arnold's ambivalent response to the modern world. As for the priority among these different causes, it would be a mistake to describe one as primary and the others as secondary, probably, for they interact in such a way that one has a primary role at one time and a secondary role at another.

Arnold resembles Carlyle in that he failed to overcome a paralyzing fear of our common humanity. But the difference between the two is great. Carlyle could not offer a creative solution to the political or social problem because of the conflict in his own nature. Arnold, on the other hand, could not solve the problem of his own nature, in part at least, because he could not solve the social problem—because he could not develop a unified view of the modern world. Carlyle's mode of adjustment to the age is to be understood in terms of the conflicts of his own personality. The conflicts in Arnold's personality are to be understood, in part at least, in terms of his mode of adjustment to the age.

Arnold's conflicting response to the modern spirit had consequences more serious, however, than the intensification of the psychic cleavage in him. It is the source of his limitation as a practical critic of society. If his lucid and luminous vision of human goals was made possible by the creative force of the middle class, his weaknesses as a critic have their source in his inability to transcend the middle-class dilemma. Arnold's advocacy of culture was an attempt to answer the needs of both sides of his nature. Through the gospel of culture he tried to convince himself that a steady advance toward perfection was possible and to assure himself at the same time that the advance would not move too fast and get out of hand. Culture was to promote the full realization of human potentialities but it was to do so without sanctioning any institutional change designed to achieve that end. Arnold's confidence in the modern spirit made culture an eloquent and moving gospel, but his distrust of the modern spirit made it an ineffectual one. The ineffectuality appears most clearly in the way, in working out his ideas of how culture should operate, Arnold permits his fear of institutional change to distort the facts of history. Throughout his exposition of the theory of culture and the critical framework that supports it, one notes that Arnold puts primary stress on the role of ideas and that he neglects, subordinates, or misrepresents the role of institutional change.

Much is to be said, to be sure, for Arnold's sense of the importance of ideas in themselves. He was one of those who try to see life "under the aspect of a distinct and illuminating idea" so that "all things become interrelated and it is no step at all from the investigation of Homer to the investigation of elementary schools."[128] "To be consequent and powerful," Arnold makes Arminius say in *Friendship's Garland,* "men must be bottomed in some vital idea or sentiment, which lends strength and certainty to their action."[129] The "happiest moments of humanity," Arnold knew, are those creative ages when the national life becomes "permeated by thought," when a fresh and vital current of ideas is abroad.[130] For Arnold the French Revolution was "the greatest, the most animating event in history" in part because of the way the masses were moved by ideas at that time. Even in his own day he believed that France was the country where the masses were most alive, because ideas, specifically the ideas of the Revolution, remained alive there as an animating force.[131] The function of the critical spirit itself, one recalls, was in Arnold's view the propagation of a current of fresh and true ideas. One can have only praise for this stress on the animating power of ideas. We should not forget, too, that Arnold's belief in the primary role of ideas was a main source of the sense of urgency we feel everywhere in his work—a sense of urgency that constitutes one source of his literary power. In his attempt to operate on the minds of his contemporaries, he believed that he was working against time.

At times, however, Arnold's sense of the primary role of ideas led him to a disparagement of action which many readers today must feel to be less praiseworthy. "To act is easy," he is fond of saying; "to think is hard."[132] Culture must not go out into the arena where men act, he insists; it must work quietly and as an inward operation.[133] As a way out of our present troubles, he says in *Culture and Anarchy,* we need not legislation, not committees, or petitions, or campaigns, but culture, which works always in the realm of the intellect and the spirit.[134] What is important is not to act and to institute, but to know what is to be acted and instituted.[135] People blame him, he says, because he does not lend a hand when action is needed: "But what if rough and coarse action, ill-calculated action, action with insufficient light, is and has for a long time been, our bane?" he replies.[136] When in the eighteen-eighties Arnold addressed himself to the Irish question, he proposed to proceed by "keeping quite in the background at present, and seeking to work on men's minds quietly rather than to bustle in Parliament and at public meetings."[137] Later, in "The Nadir of Liberalism," he remarked that it was now fifteen years "since I exhorted my young literary and intellectual friends, the lights of Liberalism, not to be rushing into the arena of politics themselves, but rather to work inwardly upon the predominant force in our politics—the great middle class—and to cure its spirit."[138]

There is little question that in this tendency to disparage action as opposed to thought, Arnold was in part rationalizing a distrust of change associated with his fear of the modern spirit. His warnings against hasty action, of course, are sensible; we are commonly confronted with situations which call, not for precipitant action, which is easy, but for unhurried meditation, which is difficult. But still more often we are faced with situations which call for a combination of thought and action, theory and practice—the kind of combination in which each activity strengthens the other.

Arnold's distrust of practical action led him to enunciate the doctrine of disinterestedness, the doctrine that the critic must be enlisted in the service of truth rather than of a practical movement or political party. In warning that commitment to the aims of a political party of the kind for which the *Edinburgh Review* and *Quarterly Review* were notorious[139] might impair the critical function, Arnold made a point to which no reasonable objection can be made. The doctrine of disinterestedness, however, has come in recent times to mean rather more than Arnold intended—with confusing results. It has come to mean that the critic should concern himself purely with esthetic values and disregard the social, political, or moral implications of literature; or it has come to mean that the critic should invariably separate himself from any attempt to find a solution for practical problems, when Arnold's intention was rather to insist that when he addresses himself to practical affairs the critic should not be in a hurry to urge this or that kind of action, that he should not feel bound to advocate the kind of action called for by a political platform, but should attempt rather to bring to bear upon the matter the best light available. In view of Arnold's distrust of practical activity these extensions of his meaning when he spoke of disinterestedness are understandable, but they represent something different from his intention nevertheless. The fact that Arnold's period was followed immediately by the period of estheticism has also been responsible, perhaps, for the shift in meaning of the term Arnold used. *Culture and Anarchy* was published in 1869, Pater's *Renaissance* in 1873. The esthetic movement has exercised a sufficiently powerful influence, it may be, so that the art-for-art's-sake tenet that the artist should not concern himself with practical affairs has been pressed back and made to apply to Arnold, whose thinking was actually very different from that of the esthetic movement.

Some scholars since Arnold's time have assumed that disinterestedness meant for him what it has come to mean for us, and have then berated him for failing in his own practice to live up to his theory. For during his best years Arnold did address himself to practical questions—questions of education, of religion, of politics. George Saintsbury gives the title "In the Wilderness" to the chapter in which he discusses Arnold's essays on political and religious questions.[140] The main theme of E. K. Brown's recent study of Arnold is that the poet did violence to his own best talents by disregarding his own rule of disinterestedness and occupying himself with the practical issues of the day.[141] Such a criticism of Arnold would appear doubly unfortunate: first, because it assumes that disinterestedness means something different from what Arnold intended; second, because even if Arnold had had the modern definition of disinterestedness in mind, we would have to commend rather than reprove him for failing to carry out his theory in his own life. It may be true that the portion of Arnold's work which is concerned mainly with practical questions does not stand up as well as the poetry and the criticism devoted to themes of more universal significance, but it does not follow that Arnold's effort to become a force in the practical affairs of the day is to be regretted. The analogy of the poet in wartime is pertinent. No one doubts that a poet's service behind a machine gun is a lesser contribution to his country than the poems he might have written if not so occupied; but it does not follow that a good poet should always stay out of combat. If the poetry is to be good perhaps the poet must be a man who at certain times is ready to give up poetry for more direct action. It might be argued, similarly, that it was precisely because Arnold had a temperament that required him at certain times to devote himself to practical affairs that his poetry and criticism not devoted to these questions so greatly move us.

We should not object, then, either to Arnold's theory of disinterestedness—a sane and temperate doctrine, on the whole—or to the way he applied it in his own life. If he could have seen that disinterestedness would come to mean that the critic should disassociate himself from practical affairs —rather than, as he intended, that he should address himself to practical affairs in a detached and philosophical manner—

we may be sure that his flexibility would have prompted him to shift stress to the side of practice. At a particular time, in a particular situation, Arnold believed that the need was for more thought and less action, but in a time when the artist has come to be widely viewed as properly inhabiting a world of his own, it would have been in keeping with Arnold's habit of mind to shift ground and insist on the need not for disinterestedness but for "interestedness."

The harmful effects of Arnold's inability to escape from the middle-class conflict lie not so much in a tendency to disparage action or in a possible one-sidedness in the doctrine of disinterestedness as in a faulty analysis of historic events and, partly in consequence of this, unworkable proposals for securing the ends which he so admirably defined. The intelligence of today must often be dumfounded by the way Arnold disregards the influence of institutions and exaggerates man's power to achieve cultural change through the agency of thought and spirit alone. To some extent our difficulty here is one we encounter in reading all the Victorians; it is the difficulty of the twentieth century, product of so many influences, sociological and psychological, which call to attention the limitations of the independent power of the mind, in appraising the thought of the nineteenth century before these influences had been brought to bear. The difficulty is especially troubling when we read Arnold, however, in part perhaps because in so many other ways his mind belongs to our time.

On occasion, it is true, Arnold does anticipate a twentieth-century view of how institutions shape man's mental and spiritual traits. One could hardly find a better account of the way the material conditions of a class determine its cultural traits than Arnold's remark that "aristocracies cannot deal with a time for intelligence; their sense is for facts, not ideas. The world of ideas is the possible, the future; the world of aristocracies is the established, the past, which has made their fortune, and which they hope to prolong."[142] Arnold even describes the "grand style" as a product of material circumstances—among them the circumstance that the class which employs it is "placed above the necessity of constantly struggling for little things."[143] But generally Arnold writes as if conscious only of the power of ideas to change institutions and not at all of the power of institutions to change ideas. He speaks as if man had it in his power through ideas alone, through the operation purely of the critical intelligence, to bring into being another age of Pericles or of Elizabeth.[144] In speaking of the relationship between religion and practical affairs, he makes much of the way "the narrow and mechanical conception of our secular business [proceeds] from the narrow and mechanical conception of our religious business,"[145] but pays no attention to the reverse process, the influence of man's secular activities upon his religious practices and beliefs. He traces the institutional changes of the Renaissance and Reformation back to spiritual causes—to "the active and animated condition of the human spirit at that time"[146]—but gives no consideration to the way these spiritual phenomena may themselves have been influenced by changes in the material conditions of life. Similarly, the causes of the French Revolution for Arnold were spiritual causes alone;[147] he does not merely neglect to mention the material causes of the Revolution—he considers them as a possible explanation and then rejects them: the motive power of the Revolution, he says, lay "in the intelligence of men, and not in their practical sense."[148] He even goes so far as to suggest that the attempt to bring about institutional changes in the Revolutionary period was a mistake; the movement of ideas that brought about the Revolution "by quitting the intellectual sphere, ran, indeed, a prodigious and memorable course, but produced no such intellectual fruit as the movement of ideas of the Renaissance, and created, in opposition to itself, what I may call an *epoch of concentration*."[149] "The mania for giving an immediate political and practical application to all these fine ideas of the reason," he concludes, "was fatal."[150]

To a generation taught to regard the ideas of the Revolution as more the result than the cause of the institutional changes brought about by "political and practical" needs, Arnold's regret that the ideas took a practical turn may well seem to belong to an Alice in Wonderland world.

Arnold's comments on contemporary events provide many instances of his exclusive concern with the influence of mind on matter and his blindness to the influence of matter on mind. He speaks of the middle-class character as if it were formed entirely by spiritual influences and appears unaware that the practical activities in which members of the middle class are engaged have anything to do with the quality of their minds. He states that the acquisitiveness of the middle class has its source in the Puritan tradition which has blinded Protestant England to the deeper values of life,[151] rather than in the way members of the middle class make their living. The provincialism and fanaticism of the middle class he describes as the consequences of an illiberal religion. The contradictions in the foreign policy pursued by the middle class he explains as a consequence not of conflicting economic interests but of a failure in Hellenism, an unsatisfactory educational system, and the influence of the dissenting ministers.[152] Even the middle-class distrust of the powerful state he explains not in terms of the economic interests which required freedom from government interference, but in terms of the Puritan heritage; for the middle class, he says, state action "became inextricably associated with the idea of a Conventicle Act, a Five-Mile Act, an Act of Uniformity. Their abhorrence of such a state-action as this they extended to state-action in general; and, having never known a beneficent and just state-power, they enlarged their hatred of a cruel and partial state-power, the only one they had ever known, into a maxim that no state-power was to be trusted."[153]

Arnold's inability to recognize the role of institutions in man's life, then—itself a consequence of his failure to escape from the middle-class dilemma—resulted in a faulty conception of how change comes about, a faulty conception, in a sense, of human nature itself. The error is to be seen not only in such examples of unhistoric history as these, but in the belief that culture, if pursued with sufficient ardor, has the power in itself, without the assistance of institutional change, to lead men toward the good society. The finest critic of his day, Arnold has enduring worth. In showing how the civilization of Victorian England fell short of fully human standards, his cool, ironic, and penetrating intelligence performed an invaluable service. In defining the goals of human aspiration —the dream that in many ways was not dreamlike but practical—he is incomparable. But he aspired to do more; he wanted to be a practical critic of his time, to show his contemporaries by what means they might as a society fulfill their best selves. In so far as he failed to do this, it was not because he was too little, but because he was too much, of his age.

Four

JOHN RUSKIN

RUSKIN'S EARLY CAREER WAS THAT OF A SINGULARLY BRILLIANT if singularly erratic art critic, one of whose most distinctive convictions was that the arts should be regarded as an expression of the society that produces them. At about forty, Ruskin shifted his main interest and henceforth wrote books chiefly about the problems of his society, though he found room in them for comments on art and, as a matter of fact, on almost every topic one could name. Ruskin's social criticism dates from about 1860 to the end of his productive life in the eighteen-eighties. Twenty-four years younger than Carlyle, and coming later in life to social criticism than Carlyle did, he reflects little of the tension and alarm that marked the period of the Reform Bill and of Chartism. Though born the year before Arnold, Ruskin was immunized by a sheltered home life, by Evangelicalism, and by his preoccupation with art from the understanding of the eighteen-forties and fifties that appears in Arnold's work. The period to which he is to be related as a social critic is the boom period of industrialism, the mid-years of the golden age of British capitalism.

Ruskin said he gave up criticism of art for criticism of

society because no man could go on painting pictures in a burning house—an observation that reminds us that the most prosperous Victorian years could impress a contemporary as anything but serene. "For my own part . . . I have seceded from the study not only of architecture, but nearly of all art; and have given myself, as I would in a besieged city, to seek the best modes of getting bread and water for its multitudes, there remaining no question, it seems to me, of other than such grave business for the time."[1] The shift in interest came at a time of personal crisis for Ruskin. It was at this time, for one thing, that he abandoned the faith in which he had been brought up. The conflict between science and religion had troubled him as early as 1851: "If only the Geologists would let me alone, I could do very well, but those dreadful hammers! I hear the clink of them at the end of every cadence of the Bible phrases."[2] When he met Holman Hunt in Venice in the sixties he declared himself an atheist, giving it as his belief that there is no eternal father and that man must be his own helper and only resource.[3] Not that Ruskin remained consistent in this view, any more than he did in any other view. Yet it is clear that Ruskin is one of the many Victorians who turned with a new seriousness to social questions when they found that traditional religious belief had failed them.

The crisis of 1860, however, was mainly an inner crisis occasioned by the belated, partial, and extremely costly revolt against the domination of that part of his own nature which had been patterned by parental influence. As with Carlyle, Ruskin's attitudes were shaped in the main by powerful internal conflicts; he did not, like Arnold, have sufficient relative integration so that the conflicts the age imposed were among the most serious that beset him. Ruskin's parents, discovering that they had a genius on their hands, had devoted themselves to his nurture with the self-dedication of people whose lives are incomplete. In their handling of the boy they combined affection and strict discipline in such a way as to attach the child to his parents with bonds that proved for many years stronger than he could sever. It was not till Ruskin was twenty-six and famous that he was allowed to go abroad for the first time without his parents—and even then it was arranged that he should be accompanied by a valet, a guide, and a traveling servant.[4] The letters that passed between Ruskin and his parents, as Amabel Williams-Ellis remarks, resemble lovers' letters in their minute analysis of misunderstandings and grievances and unintended offenses. "There is something terrible in such minuteness of memory on both sides. We seem to see two spirits handcuffed together."[5]

It is to this abnormal relationship with his parents that one must trace the unhappy story of Ruskin's unconsummated marriage, his frantic tirades against sex, which far surpass the norms even of a prudish age, and his emotional attachments, as a middle-aged man, to very young girls, the most notable example of which was his pitiable infatuation with Rose La Touche, to whom he proposed when he was forty-seven and she seventeen. Charles Eliot Norton understood well that Ruskin suffered from what today would be called neurosis, as he shows when he says that "the deepest currents of his life ran out of sight, but it was plain that they did not run calmly, and their troubled course became manifest now and then in extravagances of action and paradoxes of opinion."[6] Usually Ruskin fought against admitting any weakness in himself; often he compensated for the unconscious realization of weakness by delusions of omniscience and infallibility; yet sometimes he shows a grasp of the malady from which he suffered. When he remarks that "it seems to be the peculiar judgment-curse of modern days that all their greatest men shall be plague-struck,"[7] one has no doubt that he has himself in mind. No one can read Ruskin's writing or his biography without feeling pity for this greatly talented but tortured spirit.

R. H. Wilenski[8] regards the malady which eventually culminated in recurrent periods of insanity as manic-depressive psychosis; Louis Bragman,[9] T. M. Mitchell,[10] and Louise Nelson[11] confirm this view. In reading Ruskin one must constantly make allowances for the psychic disturbances reflected in his work. In *Fors Clavigera,* written during the seventies and early eighties, the reader learns to pay little attention when Ruskin announces that he will take up a certain subject; he seldom does so. Even the work of the sixties is marked by endless caprice and irrelevancy. The fact is that in his social criticism Ruskin was often not dealing primarily with outer reality, but was resolving tensions and releasing aggressions of his own subconscious nature. He seldom achieved that disciplined fidelity to outer fact that is indispensable for satisfactory literary construction. One must make allowances also for an arrogance that would strike the reader as intolerable if he were not aware of its neurotic origins. When Ruskin in his moods of manic exaltation offered blueprints for the total reconstruction of society, he laid down the most minute regulations as to the conduct of life in the new era. Permission to marry, for example, was to be granted publicly at village festivals held twice a year, in spring and autumn.[12] He prescribes the dress to be worn by different groups in the community, the degree of purity to be used in metals for coinage, and the stampings and inscriptions for each coin.[13] He prescribes that a bishop or overseer shall be in charge of each one hundred families and render an account for each individual.[14] Farmers, he decides, will be permitted to use the power only of animal or man, or wind and water—direct natural forces—not of machines.[15] In the new society, he says, "I will allow no man to admonish anybody, until he has previously earned his own dinner by more productive work than admonition"[16]—a rule for which much might be said, to be sure, though one cannot help thinking how much admonishing Ruskin himself was in the habit of doing though he admitted on another occasion that he "never did a stroke of work in my life worth my salt, not to mention my dinner."[17] All this apocalyptical blueprinting, however, would prove an almost intolerable exasperation to a reader unaware of its pathological origin.

One must make allowances, again, for a great amount of hostility—directed as often as not toward the reader. Ruskin was capable of great "sweetness and delicacy," of great kindness, as we see, for example, in the letter in which he offered financial help to Rossetti: "It seems to me that, amongst all the painters I know, you on the whole have the greatest genius, and you appear to me also to be—as far as I can make out—a very good sort of person. I see that you are unhappy, and that you can't bring out your genius as you should. It seems to me, then, that the proper and *necessary* thing, if I can, to make you more happy, and that I should be more really useful in enabling you to paint properly and keep your room in order than in any other way. If it were necessary for me to deny myself, or to make any mighty exertion to do this, of course it might to you be a subject of gratitude, or a question if you should accept it or not. But as I don't happen to have any other objects in life, and as I have a comfortable room and all I want in it (and more), it seems to me just as natural I should try to be of use to you as that I should offer you a cup of tea if I saw you were thirsty, and there was plenty in the tea-pot, and I had got all I wanted."[18] Yet, though he was able at times to show the finest and most delicate feeling for people, as this passage indicates, at other times Ruskin was impelled by his internal malady to lunge out savagely against those about him. He was fighting a desperate battle—a losing one, in the end—for mental security; he attacked his neighbors, his contemporaries, and his readers in an effort to save himself from inner collapse. He turns to address the workingmen of England in *Time and Tide,* only to be overcome by a storm of hatred and contempt: "Your voices are not worth a rat's squeak," he cries, "either in parliament or out of it."[19]

Ruskin used his pen "to explain away his self-indulgences and to relieve his obsessions"[20] to such an extent that he frequently lost sight of the effect he must be having on the reader. While explaining to the workingman audience the evils of an unplanned economy he says he has recently felt compelled to give a hundred pounds to this needy case and another hundred pounds to that, with the result that both he and England will suffer because he will have to give up a trip to Switzerland "to examine the junctions of the molasse sandstones and nagelfluh with the Alpine limestone."[21] Reading passages of this sort one can hardly help being more impressed with the petulant old maid in Ruskin than with the point he is supposedly making. Similarly, Ruskin illustrates the decline of European civilization by complaining of the service he has received in a Paris hotel. Breakfast comes later than in the old day, he says; when it arrives, "it looks all right at first,—the napkin, china, the solid silver sugar basin, all of the old regime. Bread, butter,—yes, of the best still. Coffee, milk,—all right too. But, at last, here is a bit of the new regime. There are no sugar-tongs; and the sugar is of beetroot, and in methodically similar cakes, which I must break with my finger and thumb if I want a small piece, and put back what I don't want for my neighbor, tomorrow."[22] Only a man pathologically absorbed in his own conflicts could cite the absence of sugar tongs in a Paris hotel as a grievance calculated to impress the English factory worker.

But the experience that gave rise to Ruskin's pathology was at the same time a source of strength in his social criticism, a criticism in some ways the most powerful produced in England in the nineteenth century. The strength of Ruskin's social criticism lies in the clarity and force with which he assails the irrationalities of the industrial system and the debasement of human nature for which he holds it responsible. Here Ruskin's magnificent intelligence, though recurrently entrammeled by obsessional drives as always, was able to work with great freedom and his incomparable gift of language was used to the finest effect. But we are constantly aware of deeper and more intimate sources of power than the rational intelligence plus command of the instrument of expression. The patterns of human relationship Ruskin had made his own in childhood had exceptional importance for him, since he had adopted them at the cost of suppressing his spontaneous self. Like Carlyle, he used an image of human relationship generated within the family—the image of an organic, tightly related, responsible society—as a criterion by which to judge the social relationships of contemporary England. The divergence between the image and the actuality gave rise to the anxiety, dismay, and fury a man feels when a conception that has neurotic importance for him is threatened. At the same time the intensity of feeling that accompanied the revolt of long-suppressed instinctual drives was diverted toward the object of immediate attack in his criticism. The tone, the emotional power, and to a great extent the ideas of Ruskin's social criticism are to be explained, then, in terms of his neurotic nature.

Comparing the Victorian spectacle of poverty amid plenty with his private image of the rationally ordered human family, Ruskin sweeps to the attack on a society where every plus sign of wealth is balanced by a minus sign of poverty, but where the pluses "make a very positive and venerable appearance in the world," while "the minuses have, on the other hand, a tendency to retire into back streets, and other places of shade,—or even to get themselves out of sight into graves."[23] "Though England is deafened with spinning wheels," he exclaims, "her people have not clothes—though she is black with digging fuel, they die of cold—and though she has sold her soul for gain, they die of hunger."[24] Comparing the ethics of the new society, in which self-interest has become a virtue, with the humane ethics he had acquired as a child, he denounces the "thrice accursed, thrice impious doctrine of the modern economist, that 'to do the best for yourself, is finally to do the best for others.' "[25] "So far as I know," he says, "there is not in history record of anything so disgraceful to the human intellect as the modern idea that the commercial text, 'Buy in the cheapest market and sell in the dearest,' represents, or under any circumstances could represent, an available principle of political economy."[26] The assertion that the predatory instinct is "one of the conditions of man's nature, and, consequently, of all arrangements of civilized society" he describes as the "most vile sentence which I have ever seen in the literature of any country or any time."[27] He reminds the reader constantly that the pursuit of material gain, which the economy views as the foundation of national welfare, is for Christianity the root of all evil.[28] Your religion, he says, tells you to love your neighbor, but "you have founded an entire science of political economy, on what you have stated to be the constant instinct of man—the desire to defraud his neighbor."[29] You "mock Heaven and its Powers, by pretending belief in a revelation which asserts the love of money to be the root of *all* evil, and declaring, at the same time, that [you are] actuated . . . in all chief national deeds and measures, by no other love."[30] "I know no previous instance in history of a nation's establishing a systematic disobedience to the first principles of its professed religion."[31]

With savage elation Ruskin strips away the humbug through which men disguise from themselves the injustices from which they profit. To those who say the poor should bear with patience the burdens placed upon them by Providence, he retorts: "You knock a man in the ditch, and then you tell him to remain content in the 'position in which Providence has placed him.'"[32] "It is the merest insolence of selfishness," he insists, "to preach contentment to a laborer who gets thirty shillings a week, while we suppose an active and plotting covetousness to be meritorious in a man who has three thousand a year."[33] When the economist justifies lavish expenditures by the rich on the ground that they give employment to the poor, Ruskin sets the record straight by asserting that the rich do not support the poor by their spending; the poor support the rich by their work: "There is something to be said in favor of the present arrangement," he adds, "but it cannot be defended in disguise; and it is impossible to do more harm to the cause of order, or the rights of property, than by endeavors . . . to revive the absurd and, among all vigorous thinkers, long since exploded notion of the dependence of the poor upon the rich."[34]

These subjects arouse in Ruskin at times an effective form of fury-tinged humor. Quoting the remark that some of the new wealth of the country is now "filtering downwards to the actual workers," for example, he asks: "But whence, then, did it filter down to us, the actual idlers?"[35] Referring to the economist's contention that payment of interest is to be regarded as a reward for abstinence, compensation for risk, and wages for the labor of superintendence, Ruskin remarks that his fifteen thousand pounds of bank stock have not brought "the slightest communication from the directors that they wished for my assistance in the superintendence of that establishment"; as for compensation for risk, "I put my money into the bank because I thought it exactly the safest place to put it in"; and as for the interest's being a reward for abstinence, "If I had not my fifteen thousand pounds of Bank Stock I should be a good deal more abstinent than I am" and "nobody would talk of rewarding me for it."[36] It is in this fashion that Ruskin disposes of the cant of the political economist. As for the economist's assertion that economic depressions are caused by overproduction, this, says Ruskin, is "accurately the most foolish thing, not only hitherto said by men, but which it is possible for men ever to say, respecting their own business. No foolish being on earth will ever be capable of saying such another foolish thing, through all the ages."[37]

Ruskin displays a great gift not only for stripping off the disguises which hide the true relationship between man and man in an industrial society but for presenting these relationships in the most graphic form. If interest, for example, is not reward for abstinence, compensation for risk, or wages for superintendence, what is it? It is a device, says Ruskin, by means of which one man gets another to do his work. Seven thousand pounds which he has in government bonds, he tells his workingman audience, entitle him to a white slip of paper with some marks on it "which gives me a right to tax you every year, and make you pay me two hundred pounds out of your wages; which is very pleasant for me; but how long will you be pleased to do so?"[38] The loans floated by the Thiers government in 1871, Ruskin says, mean "that all the poor laboring persons in France are to pay the rich idle ones five per cent annually, on the sum of eighty millions of sterling pounds, until further notice." Furthermore, the government will have to keep the army in good shape to ensure that the interest is paid, so that the poor man will be required not only to pay the interest but to support the army that compels him to pay this interest: "He must pay the cost of his own roller."[39]

If interest is a device for getting another to do one's work, wealth, according to Ruskin, equals power over men. "What is really desired, under the name of riches, is, essentially, power over men; in its simplest terms, the power of obtaining for our own advantage the labor of servant, tradesman, and artist; in wider sense, authority of directing large masses of the nation to various ends."[40] A man cannot acquire a large fortune through "fair pay for fair labor" but only "by obtaining command over the labor of multitudes of other men, and taxing it for [his] own profit."[41] It would be a good thing, Ruskin said, using the device of intentionally naïve illustration which he handled so well, if every rich man could be addressed in his youth in some such words as these: "You are likely to be maintained all your life by the labor of other men. You will have to make shoes for nobody, but some one will have to make a great many for you. You will build houses and make clothes for no one, but many a rough hand must knead clay, and many an elbow be crooked to the stitch, to keep that body of yours warm and fine. Now remember, whatever you and your work may be worth, the less your keep costs, the better. It does not cost money only. It costs degradation. You do not merely employ these people. You also tread upon them. It cannot be helped;—you have your place, and they have theirs; but see that you tread as lightly as possible, and on as few as possible."[42]

"Nearly every problem of State policy and economy, as at present understood, and practised," Ruskin says in another effective instance of naïve illustration, "consists in some device of persuading you laborers to go and dig up dinner for us reflective and aesthetical persons, who like to sit still, and think, or admire."[43] For when we get to the bottom of the matter, we will find that the inhabitants of the earth fall into two great classes. The first is the peasantry—the working people—the "original and imperial producers of turnips." Then, "waiting on them all round," is the other group, "a crowd of polite persons, modestly expectant of turnips, for some—too often theoretical—service. There is, first, the clerical person, whom the peasant pays in turnips for giving him moral advice; then the legal person, whom the peasant pays in turnips for telling him, in black letters, that his house is his own; there is, thirdly, the courtly person, whom the peasant pays in turnips for presenting a celestial appearance to him; there is, fourthly, the literary person, whom the peasant pays in turnips for talking daintily to him; and there is, lastly, the military person, whom the peasant pays in turnips for standing, with a cocked hat on, in the middle of the field, and exercising a moral influence upon the neighbors."[44]

Penetrating and impassioned as was Ruskin's criticism of contemporary society, when it came to offering a remedy his thinking became less coherent and less forceful. Often such proposals as he makes come as a bewildering anticlimax after the storm of his denunciation. He follows a dramatic picture of the way England is squandering her wealth in manufacture, for example, by asking: What can we do about it? And his answer is: With what you can spare from charity "buy ever so small a bit of ground . . . but buy it *freehold,* and make a garden of it, by hand-labor. . . . If absolutely nothing will grow in it, then have herbs carried there in pots."[45]

The principal reason for Ruskin's ineffectiveness in constructive criticism was that, like Carlyle, he was imprisoned by the psychic authoritarianism of his upbringing. It is true that at the time when he turned to social criticism, his spontaneous self was forcing its way to the surface; sometimes it carried him surprisingly far toward affirmation of the drive of the masses toward independence and a fuller life. It is in a sense extraordinary that a patrician like Ruskin should have turned away entirely from his own class to address himself to the working class. He turns to the workingmen, he says, because he knows that they "must for some time be the only body to which we can look for resistance to the deadly influence of moneyed power."[46] "What would have been the use of writing letters only for the men who have been produced by the instructions of Mr. John Stuart Mill?"[47] Ruskin's appeal to the workers was motivated in part also by the fine feeling he was capable of displaying on occasion for ordinary humanity. One recalls the way he encouraged stonemasons to carve what they would on the walls of the Oxford Museum—an attractive contrast, as William Gaunt remarks, with Whistler's reluctance to let the ordinary workman do so much as mix paints for the decoration of a room.[48]

But Ruskin could never for long think of the free drives of man's nature as anything but dangerous. He returned always to the conviction that just as the individual must master his instinctive impulses, so people in general must be held in check by a strict, if kind, authority. Unable to construct an image of the good society except in the guise of the wise paternalism of his home, Ruskin could not, save for sporadic flashes of insight, consider a democratic solution to the problems of Victorian society; he reverted instead to the image of a hierarchy where each man gives orders to those below him and in turn carries out in obedience the wishes of captain, leader, bishop, or king. For those who did not fit into such a scheme, repression or punishment was the only treatment. Like Carlyle, Ruskin regards the criminal not with understanding but with the same vindictiveness as he directs toward his own unsanctioned impulses. Criminals, he says, "are partly men, partly vermin; what is human in them you must punish—what is vermicular, abolish."[49] The worst misleaders of the people, he says, are those who say: "Stand up for your rights—get your division of living—be sure that you are as well off as others, and have what they have!—don't let any man dictate to you—have not you all a right to your opinion? —are you not all as good as everybody else?—let us have no governors, or rather—let us all be free and alike."[50] "My own teaching has been, and is," he repeats, "that Liberty, whether in the body, soul, or political estate of man, is only another word for Death, and the final issue of Death, putrefaction."[51]

Because Ruskin often wrote on impulse and said whatever happened to be uppermost in his mind at the moment, one can find almost any view in his work. "Ruskin calendars," says R. H. Wilenski, "can be compiled by Tories, Fascists, and Communists, by photographic painters and Cubist artists, by Chauvinists and Pacifists, by parsons and agnostics. All can claim him as their man."[52] But the dominant point of view is an authoritarian one—and in this fact lies the source of his failure as a constructive critic. The only workable solution for the problems Ruskin faced was increased democracy. In the context in which be wrote, an authoritarian gospel had either to be ineffectual or, as an anticipation of twentieth-century fascism, vicious. Perhaps there is reason to rejoice that in his attempt at constructive criticism Ruskin was as ineffectual as he was.

Aware as he necessarily became of the inadequacy of his constructive proposals, Ruskin resorted commonly to an appeal for individual reform. F. W. Bateson's comment that "the evils the Victorians denounced were always individual, and the 'heart,' the conscience, was always their cure"[53] applies to Ruskin even more than to Carlyle or Arnold. Ruskin, like Carlyle, writes constantly in such a way as to imply that social problems have their source in personal ethics and can be solved through an appeal to the individual conscience. He says, for example, that competition in commerce is caused by personal jealousy,[54] and appears not to have considered that personal jealousy might be caused by competition in commerce. He censures businessmen for acquisitiveness and workingmen for shiftlessness; "The masters cannot bear to let any opportunity of gain escape them, and frantically rush at every gap and breach in the walls of Fortune, raging to be rich, and affronting, with impatient covetousness, every risk of ruin; while the men prefer three days of violent labor, and three days of drunkenness, to six days of moderate work and wise rest."[55] That the structure of society, rather than personal weakness, may make the businessman acquisitive and the worker shiftless Ruskin appears not to consider. He reads the businessmen lectures on how they should interest themselves, not in profit, but in the purity of the product and the welfare of their employees.[56] "It is no more [the manufacturer's] function to get profit for himself . . . than it is a clergyman's function to get his stipend."[57] That a manufacturer may sacrifice both the purity of his product and his employees' welfare to profit not because he wants to but because he must, Ruskin again appears not to consider.

We can see today more clearly than anyone could see in Ruskin's time that the economic practices of the day were determined by the evolving structure of society rather than by any set of thinkers. The role of the economists, at best, was to give a theoretical justification to practices which men adopted because they had little choice. Those who cited the authority of the economists in support of their actions were finding an ideological justification for what they were impelled to do by circumstance. But Ruskin, permitting himself to believe that everything could be changed if one could only reach the individual conscience, tried to deliver his contemporaries from the false teaching of the economists. "When I accuse Mill of being the root of nearly all immediate evil among us in England," he said, "I am in earnest."[58] The lack of cogency in much of Ruskin's writing has its source in this mistaken assumption that abstract principles, rather than the necessities of an evolving society, determine the form of economic conduct.

Even when writing about war, Ruskin assumes that the problem can be solved by an appeal to the individual understanding or conscience. He uses all the rhetorical devices at his command to exhibit the absurdity of modern warfare. The nations today are like neighbors, he says, who instead of enjoying one another's society, employ their ingenuity and money in trying to excel one another in the manufacture of steel traps with which each hopes to catch the other if he ventures to trespass.[59] For England to spend a hundred and fifty times as much money on arms as on art, again, is as if a private gentleman should spend 164 pounds on pictures and then think nothing of spending 24,000 pounds for private detectives to watch the shutters.[60] The "essential character" of every war can be understood, says Ruskin, if we think of it as a fight between men of neighboring counties. The Franco-Prussian War of 1871, for example, might be regarded as a struggle between Lancashire and Yorkshire for the line of the Ribble. In the course of the quarrel Lancashire demands from Yorkshire the townships of Giggleswick and Wigglesworth. Over this question the men of both counties pour out their wealth and their blood.[61] We see today that the wars of the nineteenth century, like its economic conduct, were brought about by forces originating in the structure of society rather than by any failure of the intellect to grasp their absurdity or by any atrophy of the private sense of justice; they were fought despite the fact that people saw them to be wasteful and wrong, not, as Ruskin's rhetoric implies, because they failed to see this.

It may seem unfair in a sense to take Ruskin to task for

belonging to his century rather than to ours. It was much less easy for Ruskin's contemporaries than for ours to see that by the mid-nineteenth century British society had developed a dynamic partly independent of men's conscious desires, with the result that God-fearing men paid their employees starvation wages, men privately disposed to coöperative enterprise engaged in destructive forms of competition, selfless men devoted their lives to acquisitive accumulation, and peaceloving men supported policies designed to protect investments, commandeer sources of raw material, and safeguard lines of trade by force of arms. Yet it is not only from the vantage point of the mid-twentieth century that Ruskin's failure to take account of this independent social dynamic becomes apparent. "Though in relation to nature he is a true naturalist," *The Spectator* said of Ruskin in 1877, "in relation to human nature [he] has in him nothing at all of the human naturalist. It never occurs to him apparently that here, too, are innumerable principles of growth which are quite independent of the will of man, and that it becomes the highest moralist to study humbly where the influence of human will begins and where it ends, instead of rashly and sweepingly condemning, as due to a perverted morality, what is in innumerable cases a mere inevitable result of social structure."[62] Ruskin's failure to apprehend rightly the relationship between the individual and society could not be better formulated. How far Ruskin was from accepting this form of criticism as pertinent may be seen from his infuriated reply: "England at this time has no 'social structure,' whatsoever; but is a mere heap of agonizing human maggots, scrambling and sprawling over each other for any manner of rotten eatable thing they can get a bite of."[63] Whistler, with characteristic malice, once said that the artists thought Ruskin a great political economist and the economists thought him a great artist.[64] One would be inclined to agree with the economists that Ruskin lacked capacity for the subject he was dealing with—provided, of course, that such agreement did not imply that the orthodox economists had greater competence.

Ruskin's appeal to the individual conscience prompted him to write many purple passages of somewhat facile inspirationalism—passages in which he evidently supplied the age with something it needed. It was this aspect of Ruskin's work that Prince Leopold selected for praise in a speech delivered in 1879. Ruskin had shown the English artisans, the Prince said, how they could draw "the full measure of instruction and happiness from this wonderful world on which both rich and poor gaze alike." His great lesson is "that the highest wisdom and the highest pleasure need not be costly or exclusive, but may be almost as cheap and as free as air,—and that the greatness of a nation must be measured, not by her wealth or her apparent power, but by the degree in which all her people have learnt to gather from the world of books, of Art, and of Nature, a pure and ennobling joy."[65] The passages of vague uplift to which the Prince refers now embarrass more than they inspire. In making an anthology of Ruskin selections fit to endure, one would omit every one of them.

No one can fail to be impressed with Ruskin's account of the manner in which his own society had lost its bearings. Yet the deepest impression made by Ruskin's social criticism as a whole is one of the pathos of an immense and tragic failure. It was a failure of which he himself was keenly aware. Unable either to shelve or to solve the problems of his age, he fell victim, he told Charles Eliot Norton, to a "daily maddening rage."[66] He gives way to "the unmeasured anger against human stupidity" which can often be, as John Morley finely says, "one of the most provoking forms of that stupidity."[67] He rages at the "money theory" of modern times, which "corrupts the Church, corrupts the household, destroys honor, beauty and life throughout the universe. It is *the* death incarnate of Modernism, and the so-called science of its pursuit is the most cretinous, speechless, paralyzing plague that has yet touched the brains of mankind."[68] He takes the preachers to task for giving support to Mill and to Mammon.[69] He lashes at his countrymen for letting "the destinies of twenty myriads of human souls" be determined by "the chances of an enlarged or diminished interest in trade."[70] His invectives become increasingly violent till they reach the point of hysteria: "We English, as a nation, know not, and care not to know, a single broad or basic principle of human justice. We have only our instincts to guide us. We will hit anybody who hits us. We will take care of our own families and our own pockets; and we are characterized in our present phase of enlightenment mainly by rage in speculation, lavish expenditure on suspicion or panic, generosity whereon generosity is useless, anxiety for the souls of savages, regardlessness of those of civilized nations, enthusiasm for liberation of blacks, apathy to enslavement of whites, proper horror of regicide, polite respect for populicide, sympathy with those whom we can no longer serve, and reverence for the dead, whom we have ourselves delivered to death."[71] Sometimes the invective turns into a shriek of loathing for "this yelping, carnivorous crowd, mad for money and lust, tearing each other to pieces, and starving each other to death, and leaving heaps of their dung and ponds of their spittle on every palace floor and altar stone."[72] When we read Ruskin we are often made to feel, as Leslie Stephen said, that we are "listening to the cries of a man of genius, placed in a pillory to be pelted by a thick-skinned mob, and urged by a sense of his helplessness to utter the bitterest taunts he can invent."[73]

Five

JAMES THOMSON

"THE CITY OF DREADFUL NIGHT" CREATES A MOOD OF SOMBER and unrelieved desolation. Thomson's purpose in writing the poem, he said, was to tell the whole truth to the few who were ready to understand him—the truth that only those have a chance for happiness who are willing to befool themselves as to the conditions of human life, that these conditions for those who have the courage to face them honestly are of unattenuated horror. The poem speaks directly to many people in our troubled age. While it cannot be considered a representative Victorian poem, it embodies a trend in Victorian experience that was never far below the surface. Here the pessimism that shows itself intermittently in Tennyson, Arnold, Carlyle, and Ruskin, and that was to appear in fuller statement in the work of Fitzgerald, Hardy, and Housman, receives its dominant and richly decorated expression.

What were the sources of Thomson's momentous record of woe? In part, surely, Thomson the man was the tormented victim of some inner and purely personal disorder. He spoke of himself as "mad with self-consciousness of guilt and woe, accurst, his breast seared with remorse, his brain gnawed on by hopeless doubt and anxiety."[1] Imogene B. Walker, in a recent study of Thomson, conjectures that the sense of guilt which tortured him may have had its source in his rejection of religious belief,[2] but one would suppose that the truest origin must have lain rather in some repression of instinctual drives that took place long before he reached the age of conceptual thinking. Though Thomson was in many ways normal enough, and was capable even of a "profound relish for existence,"[3] one need have no hesitation in attributing mainly to psychic abnormality his habitual melancholy, his alcoholism, and his suicidal impulses—not to speak of the philosophical pessimism of his great poem.

In dealing with an author in whom the element of abnormality is beyond dispute, care is needed not to put too much—or too little—stress on the morbid element. If Thomson was abnormal he was at the same time a person whose response to nineteenth-century society merits serious study, as does that of Carlyle and Ruskin; the abnormal trends in his personality served in part to throw into sharper relief experience that he truly and rightly apprehended. But at the same time one cannot entirely discount the element of abnormality. One must be prepared for distortion as well as intensification of experience, and for the kind of overreaction that is as likely to misrepresent the trends of the time as to throw them into distinct focus.

While attempting to maintain this guarded attitude, then, let us try to form an estimate of the general human significance—the nonneurotic significance, so to speak—of Thomson's pessimism. What causes, apart from the principal one—his subconscious need for self-injury—account for it? With what trends in Victorian thought and experience is it to be associated?

Since a man's philosophy is the product of the whole of his experience, everything that happened to Thomson is relevant to an attempt to explain his pessimism. The religious fanaticism of his Irvingite mother, his years in an orphanage, the death of his fiancée Matilda Weller, his abandonment of religious belief, his rather dismal years as army schoolmaster, his association with the Secularist leader Charles Bradlaugh—all these experiences have a bearing upon the problem. As to which of these influences were of major importance, the biographers are uncertain. H. S. Salt believes that the death of Matilda Weller was the principal cause of Thomson's melancholy: "We are compelled to believe . . . that it was the death of this young girl that, above all other single circumstances, fostered and developed the malady to which Thomson was predisposed, and that in this sense, at least, it was the cause of his subsequent despondency."[4] In this view Bertram Dobell concurs: "It may . . . be taken as certain that the death of Matilda Weller was the chief cause of Thomson's unhappiness. . . . I believe that if she had lived to become the wife of Thomson, he might very well have got the better of his melancholy disposition."[5] In an unpublished poem summarized by Dobell in his introduction to Thomson's poems, the poet himself attributed his lifelong unhappiness to Matilda's death. But the influences of which one is conscious are not necessarily the most significant ones. Though Thomson undoubtedly wrote sincerely in the poem in question, one can hardly help regarding it as a romantic falsification to attribute habitual melancholia in a mature man to the sense of loss occasioned by the death of a childhood sweetheart.

Paul Elmer More regards Thomson's pessimism as the logical outgrowth of the philosophic naturalist's surrender to the flux of experience.[6] Lord David Cecil, similarly, explains Thomson's pessimism, like that of Arnold, Fitzgerald, and Hardy, as in the main a response to the loss of religious belief. Such explanations may well seem sufficient to those committed to a mode of belief analogous to the one Thomson had renounced, but others will think of contemporaries of Thomson—Swinburne, William Morris, or Samuel Butler, for example—for whom loss of faith was anything but depressing.

Yet clearly in the attempt to form an estimate of the causes of Thomson's pessimism we must regard his response to the breakdown of belief as of primary importance, even if it is not, as Paul Elmer More and David Cecil assert, a sufficient explanation in itself. In "The City of Dreadful Night" Thomson writes of the horror of a universe "that has no purpose, heart or mind or will," a universe governed by "Necessity Supreme":

> This little life is all we must endure,
> The grave's most holy peace is ever sure,
> We fall asleep and never wake again.

The poem is filled with curses against the "malignant and implacable" God who does not exist, "the creator of all woe and sin"—curses that reflect the embittered mood of a man cast out from belief for which he hungers emotionally.

In viewing as intellectually untenable beliefs for which he retains an emotional need, Thomson is representative of a typical Victorian phenomenon. "From the bottom of his heart he wanted to believe in God, in immortality, in the essential goodness of mankind; but his observations of the world and the implications which his analytical mind saw in those observations abundantly fed the ever-growing doubt which bit by bit undermined, weakened, and eventually killed his faith."[7] Living at a time when Darwinism and Biblical criticism had for many shattered the foundations of belief, he came to regard religion as "a hideous mockery and an impossible delusion,"[8] but he could not reconcile himself to a purposeless universe. Like other Victorians, he could not throw the problem off; poems like "Vane's Story" and "To Our Ladies of Death" and prose pieces like "A Lady of Sorrow" and "Sayings of Sigvat" show how perpetually he revolved these questions in his mind. Everywhere in his work one sees how "the Christian conscience survived in him to torment the skeptic."[9]

Arnold, Tennyson, Clough, Fitzgerald, Hardy—these among

how many less renowned—were tormented by the same conflict between an emotional need for belief and the testimony of the intellect which made belief untenable. The intellect led all of them toward the conviction—to quote from the well-known passage in Bertrand Russell's "A Free Man's Worship" —that "man is the product of causes which had no prevision of the end they were achieving; that his origin, his growth, his hopes and fears, his loves and his beliefs, are but the outcome of accidental collocations of atoms . . ."[10] This view they could not accept emotionally and could not reject intellectually. "Unable to hold their faith, they were unable to relinquish it and were tormented by their indecision."[11] They could not "stop worrying about God, even when [they] had become fully convinced that God was not worrying about [them]."[12]

But in one important way Thomson's response to the religious problem differs from that of the typical Victorian. For most men of Thomson's period loss of faith was painful because religion served as an apparently almost indispensable prop for values, psychological and social, which they were unwilling to abandon. Psychologically, religion provided sanctions for the restraints imposed by the established morality; the loss of these sanctions, it seemed, would lead to the moral anarchy of uninhibited appetite. "If you were to destroy in mankind the belief in immortality," they might have said with Ivan in *The Brothers Karamazov*, "not only love but every living force maintaining the life of the world would at once be dried up. Moreover, nothing then would be immoral, everything would be lawful, even cannibalism. . . . For every individual, like ourselves, who does not believe in God or immortality, the moral law of nature must immediately be changed into the exact contrary of the former religious law, and . . . egoism, even to crime, must become, not only lawful but even recognized as the inevitable, the most rational, even honorable outcomes of his position."[13] What Tennyson foresaw as a consequence of loss of faith, similarly, "was not his own extinction, nor even the ultimate extinction of human life on earth; he feared that if men ceased to believe in the immortality of the soul all that he valued in this present life would perish, morality would crumble, and man reel back into the brute."[14]

But for the typical Victorian the psychological function of religion was perhaps less important than its social function. It was because religion provided sanctions for a view of society which he felt unable to surrender that he adjusted himself with such difficulty to the loss of faith. To confirm the point that religion was valued, though not always consciously, for its social function, one needs only to recall that the great religious revival of the first half of the nineteenth century was a social phenomenon almost as much as it was a religious one. Both Tractarianism and Evangelicalism fortified with religious sanctions men who were determined to resist the force of social change which stemmed from the French Revolution. Religion enabled these men to affirm that the change needed in society was not institutional but personal, not economic but ethical. Man's duty, according to the religious view, was not to tamper with the existing order, but to bear without protest the burden placed upon him, to live a sober life, and look forward to a reward beyond the grave. At a time when the established order was more gravely threatened than it had been since the seventeenth century, religion taught that protest against the established order was misguided and iniquitous. The theologian might not always respond to questions about the common weal, as John Morley petulantly complained that he did, by telling you "something about the sacred fowls or the Thirty-nine Articles, about sacramental churches, or the aspect of the sacrificial entrails,"[15] but he was generally of the opinion, nevertheless, that tinkering with the established order would not help solve the social problem. Bertrand Russell dismisses the Tractarians as in a category with "men who find the modern world so painful that they seek escape from present reality in opium, fairy tales, or the invention of a Golden Age in the past. They are not sinister, but only lacking in the robustness required in order to think useful thoughts."[16] But by condemning as irreligious every attempt to solve the problems of the age through a change in the structure of society, the Tractarians performed an important social role. Not only the Tractarians, but all sections of organized religion, we are reminded, were opposed to Robert Owen's experiments in coöperative enterprise.[17] *Fraser's Magazine* quite candidly gave it as a reason for preserving the established church that it served as a bulwark of the established order.[18] Even Kingsley admitted that "We have used the Bible as if it were a mere special constable's handbook, an opium dose for keeping beasts of burden patient while they are being overloaded"—and so supplied Karl Marx with one of his best-known phrases.[19] There can be little doubt that theologians were unwilling to give up the idea of eternal punishment in part because of the social utility of the belief. When Lord Westbury, in exonerating two authors of *Essays and Reviews,* "dismissed Hell with costs, and took away from the orthodox their last hope of everlasting damnation,"[20] there were many who felt that the decision placed the established social order in jeopardy.

Throughout the nineteenth century, as a matter of fact, both conservatives and radicals spoke frankly about the social role of religious belief. In *Rocks Ahead,* written in the same decade as "The City of Dreadful Night," W. R. Greg names the breakdown of religious belief, along with England's industrial decline and the threat of political supremacy on the part of the "lower classes," as one of the three dangers confronting England. In a time when most intelligent men are skeptics and the best workmen nonbelievers, he says, society would appear to have forfeited one of its principal safeguards against social change.[21] A common view in the working class in the sixties and seventies, we are told, was that parsons were hypocrites and religion a device to strengthen the existing order of society.[22] Even the Christian Socialist movement of

F. D. Maurice, Charles Kingsley, and J. M. Ludlow served in some degree to direct revolutionary energies into innocuous channels. To be sure, the Christian Socialists sincerely hoped to modify the industrial system. The leaders had strong feelings about the evils of competition: "Competition is put forth as the law of the universe," said Maurice. "That is a lie. The time has come for us to declare that it is a lie, by word and deed."[23] But in their efforts to change economic practice the Christian Socialists were too innocent to achieve significant results. The Society for the Promotion of Working Men's Associations, which the Christian Socialists founded, "contained the necessary reactionary element which is the usual accompaniment of ideals formulated away from the real heart of an economic movement."[24] Maurice's prospectus for a tailors' coöperative, as quixotic a document as the century produced, gives the measure of Christian Socialist impracticality in economic affairs: "To call men to repentance first of all, and then also, as it seems to me, to give them the opportunity of showing their repentance and bringing forth fruits of it. This is my idea of a Tailors' Association."[25] Despite the intentions of its leaders, then, the Christian Socialist movement, founded as it was in the climactic year of Chartism, served mainly to provide a conservative alternative to Chartist objectives. When Stewart Headlam revived the movement with the Guild of St. Matthew in 1877 in an effort to combine high church principles with the theories of Henry George, Christian Socialism served once again to direct the revived revolutionary pressures of this later period into safe channels.[26]

When one recalls in this way the social role of religion throughout the nineteenth century, one can readily see how men might find it difficult to adjust to the loss of faith because it threatened to deprive them of sanctions for a certain outlook on society. If psychologically loss of faith threatened moral anarchy, socially it threatened a civic anarchy in which man would seek to fulfill his demands upon society without the restraint of moral principle. It is only by referring in this way to the social implications of the loss of faith that one can explain why it was that invariably those who suffered the greatest agony over the breakdown of belief were precisely those who were most deeply attached to the established order. There is a logical connection, for example, between Tennyson's horror of the "red fool-fury of the Seine" and his tortured unwillingness to follow his intellectual convictions in the direction of agnosticism.

To affirm that certain Victorians defended religious belief in part because of its social utility—or to put it crudely because it was "a dodge for keeping the poor quiet"[27]—is not necessarily to imply that they were hypocrites. Often enough, to be sure, Victorian social history makes one think of Bertrand Russell's remark that "when well-fed people tell the poor that they ought to have souls above the cravings of the belly, there is something nauseous and hypocritical about the whole performance."[28] Those who attached themselves to belief primarily because of its social usefulness necessarily manifested something of the insincerity which was, according to Hugh Kingsmill, "the skeleton in all these Victorian cupboards, and the charge which each Victorian, his back firmly against his own cupboard, would hurl most readily against his enemy of the moment."[29] Yet the insincerity was largely unconscious. Belfort Bax noticed the way people would give away their view that religion served as a prop to the social order by incidental remarks about how society, if it were not for religion, would fall apart; he believed that this consideration was the main reason for the attachment of middle-class people to religious belief; but he was convinced that the motivation worked unconsciously and that if there was any hypocrisy involved it was an unconscious hypocrisy.[30] We are dealing here, as a matter of fact, with a phenomenon not unlike that of the seventeenth century, another period when religious and social issues were inextricably intermingled. In fighting for religious freedom the Puritans were at the same time fighting for a new social order, but no one—except, of course, for their outright enemies, like the author of *Hudibras*—would accuse them of insincerity for that reason. Similarly the Victorians, in fighting to maintain religious belief at a time when it was threatened on all sides, were at the same time fighting for the stability of the established order. But they were probably on the whole no more insincere than were the Puritans. Mixture of motives of this sort is part of the normal and inevitable order of experience.

Thomson differed from the typical Victorian, however, in that, while the psychological role of religion was important to him, its social role was of no concern to him at all. Thomson was not one of those who were tortured by loss of faith because of a conscious or unconscious sense that religion was an indispensable support to the established order. He was not committed to the established order. In his early twenties he had thrown in his lot with Charles Bradlaugh and the Secularist party and he remained opposed to most of the established values of his society to the end of his life. If for those who felt committed to the existing order the normal response to the breakdown of belief was one of anxiety and fear, the normal response for those who stood apart from this society and advocated a change in institutions was one of ready acquiescence, relief, or even joyous emancipation. Neither the Chartists of the thirties and forties nor the socialists of the eighties and nineties experienced any difficulty in adjusting themselves to a secularist outlook. Writing in 1849 Henry Hetherington states that he does not believe in God and that he regards death as an eternal sleep. Like Shelley, he views religion—"priestcraft and superstition"—as the great obstacle to human progress. His statement of belief gives no hint that he experienced any difficulty in adjusting himself to such views as these.[31] For William Morris, who came to regard himself as a "pagan" or "atheist,"[32] renunciation of the belief that in college days had been fervid enough to tempt him to consider the church as a vocation appears to have occasioned nothing of the anxiety that for so many

Victorians was the normal experience. The agnostics of the seventies, as Frances Wentworth Knickerbocker says, were by no means all sad men like Clough or Arnold; many of them were hopeful, vehement men who threw themselves with ardor into social reform and public service.[33] Swinburne's enthusiasm for social regeneration was accompanied by an exultant rejection of religious dogma.

But Thomson belongs no more with the joyous iconoclasts than he does with the anxious defenders of the existing order. Though he broke with the institutions of his time, he felt nothing of the glad release of men like Hetherington or Morris; he experienced instead the continuous anguish that afflicted men for whom religion was associated with indispensable social values. To understand how it was that he could detach himself from the established order as radically as Morris and yet suffer all the anguish of Tennyson, one must consider the character of the Secularist movement with which he was for so long identified.

Thomson first contributed to the *National Reformer* in 1860, when he was twenty-six, and after 1862 he occupied a room in the home of Charles Bradlaugh, the Secularist party leader. He contributed steadily to the *National Reformer* till the time of his break with Bradlaugh in 1875, at which time he had only seven more years to live. From his twenty-sixth to his forty-first year, then, Thomson lived in the closest association with the leading member of the "three persons and no God"[34] who controlled the Secularist party, and contributed regularly to its weekly newspaper. The Secularists described themselves as adopting "reason instead of faith, science instead of revelation, nature instead of providence, work instead of worship and prayer," and as holding "that humanity, instead of divinity, should occupy the thought of men and command their service."[35] Charles Bradlaugh, an atheist and a republican, preached the Secularist creed with something of Shelley's ardor; his aim was the regeneration of society and he believed that the Secularist program was adequate to achieve that end. His followers were among the Hyde Park demonstrators of 1867—those demonstrators whom Matthew Arnold would like to have hurled from the Tarpeian Rock—and were the most militant supporters of the antimonarchical agitation of 1870-73.[36]

But the program of the Secularist movement did not answer the needs of any large group of people, and the movement was bound therefore soon to fail. Bradlaugh preached a renovated Shelleyism long after the time when Shelley's ideas had a chance to move society. The Secularist agitation coincided, moreover, with the period when nineteenth-century British society had achieved its greatest stability. The stir of Chartism had long died down; the new period of Socialism had not begun—though its moment was at hand. The trade unions were now more conservative than they had been before or were to be later. The propaganda of the "Steam Intellect Society" had at last produced results, with the consequence that young trade unionists had it as an objective "to be calm, prudent, temperate and enlightened—the qualities their seniors [had] seemed most notably to lack."[37]

While it is true, as was pointed out earlier, that popular unrest prompted Disraeli to carry through the Second Reform Bill, it may well also be true, as G. D. H. Cole says, that he was willing to do this only "because it was obvious to all that the working class had abandoned its revolutionary aspirations and could safely be trusted with the vote."[38] Within a few years all this was to be changed. The period of stabilization ended and the period of economic depression and social unrest began. The theoretical inadequacies of the Secularist movement now revealed themselves in the way the movement collapsed when brought into conflict with the superior appeal of the Socialist program. Shaw tells that the tone of the Zetetical Society, which he joined in 1879, "was strongly individualistic, atheistic, Malthusian, Ingersollian, Darwinian, and Herbert Spencerian. Huxley, Tyndall, and George Eliot were on the shelves of all the members. . . . Socialism was regarded as an exploded fallacy of Robert Owen's; and nobody dreamt that within five years Marxist Socialism would snatch away all the younger generation, and sweep the Dialectical and Zetetical Societies into the blind cave of eternal night."[39] By the beginning of the eighties most of Bradlaugh's followers had abandoned Secularism and were to be found in the radical clubs where British socialism was born,[40] many of them having discovered, as did Edward Aveling, "that Socialism was the necessary constructive correlative of the purely negative and destructive Secularism."[41]

It goes without saying that Thomson was sincere in his support of the objectives of the Secularist party. The evidence against belief in God was to him incontrovertible, and like Hetherington and Shelley he was convinced that the influence of organized religion was pernicious. The prose satire "Bumble, Bumbledon, Bumbleism"—where Bumble serves as a synonym for Arnold's Philistine—gives the measure of his antipathy toward middle-class values. The antimonarchical sentiments in poems like "Our Congratulations on the Recovery of His Royal Highness" and "L'Ancien Régime" are unquestionably genuine. He responded with sympathy to the independence movements of his time, as we see in poems like "Garibaldi Revisiting England," "A Polish Insurgent," and "Despotism Tempered by Dynamite"—a poem denouncing the tyranny of the Czar. He was far from accepting the official version of England's wars; the Crimean War he described as "a mere selfish haggle for the adjustment of the balance of power, badly begun and meanly finished,"[42] and he referred to what H. S. Salt terms "the more recent exploits of Jingoism" as "brutally iniquitous battue-wars against tribes of ill-armed savages."[43] Yet while Thomson's convictions coincided with those of the Secularists sufficiently so that he was able sincerely to support the movement, he remained in some ways curiously detached from it. He was committed intellectually only, "for his intense individuality, coupled with his almost cynical disbelief in the possibilty of any real progress, must always have prevented his giving himself heart and soul to a 'cause.' He worked, as he himself avowed, on the side of liberty and free thought, not because he believed in the ultimate triumph of these principles, but simply because he was prompted thereto by a natural instinct, and inclination. His hatred of all fuss and sham, and his impatience of the occasional 'clap-trap' and false sentiment not wholly separable from any popular movement, made him at times a sarcastic critic of his own party no less than of his adversaries."[44] For him the "supreme merit" of the *National Reformer* consisted, he said, "in the fact that I can say in it what I like how I like; and I know not another periodical in Britain which would grant me the same liberty or license."[45] But emotionally he was convinced that the Secularist movement would accomplish nothing. It was "useless and irrational to confide in any schemes for the improvement of the human race," he said.[46] He was "a disbeliever in all human progress, and, ardent admirer though he was of Shelley's character and writings, he could not subscribe to the cardinal doctrine of Shelley's faith —the perfectibility of man, since it seemed to him that if there is any advance in intellectual well-being, it is an advance in a circle, with the result that after centuries of earnest labor, and seemingly forward movement, the latest condition of the civilized race is much the same as the earliest."[47] "He denied the reality of progress in the world," says G. W. Foote; "there was revolution, but no forward movement; the balance of evil and good remained through all changes unchanged; eventually the human race, with all its hopes and fears, its virtues and crimes, its triumphs and failures, would be swept into oblivion."[48] Writing to George Eliot, Thomson says that while he respects those who have striven to alleviate the conditions of man's existence, he "cannot see that all their efforts have availed much against the primal curse of existence."[49]

Thomson supported the Secularist movement, then, with intellectual sincerity but without emotional conviction. "I don't think that there's a pin to choose between [Bradlaugh's] opinions and my own," he said; "only while he considers his opinions of the utmost importance, and is unwearied in the profitable task of converting the world to them, I care very little for mine, and don't believe the world capable of being benefited much by having any opinion whatever preached to it."[50] The break with Bradlaugh, when at last it came, was no doubt a consequence of the incompatibility in temperament between the skeptical Thomson and the idealist-partisan Bradlaugh, as H. S. Salt suggests.[51] For Thomson, regarding "all proselytism as useless and absurd,"[52] did not conceal his antipathy toward propagandists.[53] "In our time and country," he wrote in *Indolence—a Moral Essay*, "we have a plague of busy-bodyism, certainly more annoying and perhaps more noxious than the plague of idleness. One comes across many earnest and energetic characters who are no longer men, but simply machines for working out missions."[54] Thomson's *Proposals for the Speedy Extinction of Evil and Misery* is a Swiftian satire on reformers, for which he employed as epigraph this quotation from Leopardi: "But the lofty spirits of my century discovered a new, and as it were divine counsel: for not being able to make happy on earth any one person, they ignored the individual, and gave themselves to seek universal felicity; and having easily found this, of a multitude singly sad and wretched they make a joyous and happy people."[55] Thomson was not sorry when he found he was being crowded out of the *National Reformer:* "I'm always willing to give way, especially when doing so saves me from writing nonsense."[56]

Thomson was a man, then, who for many years identified himself with a reform movement which he regarded as essentially futile. Every day men join socially sanctioned movements without any particular emotional conviction, but those who support movements which, like Secularism, are the object of general obloquy are usually motivated by a zeal for reform strong enough to counterbalance the penalties that such support entails. No doubt Thomson refused to let himself believe in the efficacy of Secularism and of other "schemes for the improvement of the human race" in part because his neurotic need for self-injury disbarred him from any sort of hopeful outlook on life. But his sense of the impracticality of Secularism may have stemmed also from a just discernment that this was in fact a cause that could not succeed. Thomson's fine intelligence, it may be, enabled him to see the actuality that Bradlaugh missed because of his propagandist's capacity for self-delusion. When Thomson told himself that belief in Necessity compelled him to regard all reform movements as "useless and irrational,"[57] one suspects that Necessity was serving as rationalization of a conviction, to which his clear-sightedness led him, that the particular reform movement with which he was associated was doomed. If he had had a feebler intelligence, or if he had been of healthier mental disposition, he might have adopted the illusions of the other Secularists; but the combination of an exacting intellect and a constitutional inability to cultivate flattering illusions, deprived him of hope.

We do not get a clear perception of Thomson's predicament if we adopt the view of Paul Elmer More, Lord David Cecil, and others that the loss of faith in itself provides a key to his pessimism. Many of Thomson's contemporaries found themselves well able to get along without faith. That most men require some kind of affirmative philosophy, however, remains true. Thomson was deprived of one kind of affirmative philosophy by the breakdown of religious belief. Since he had no commitments to the established order, there was no necessary reason why he should have experienced the agony felt by men for whom religion was associated with a conservative social outlook. A decade or two earlier, or a few years later, he might well have found himself engaged in a realistic struggle for the transformation of society—a struggle that would have supplied him with the ingredients of an affirmative philosophy of a different kind. In the sixties and seventies, however, the only movement with which he found it possible to associate was one that only men with a greater capacity for self-delusion than Thomson possessed could support with conviction. Thomson's pessimism, then, is to be regarded not simply as a consequence of personal neurosis, not simply as a consequence of the breakdown of belief in the nineteenth century, but as the consequence also of a moment in history when for a man of his kind of integrity no constructive social philosophy was available.

Six

DANTE GABRIEL ROSSETTI

DANTE GABRIEL ROSSETTI (1828-82) WAS BORN FOUR YEARS before James Thomson and died in the year of Thomson's death. In so far as we are to consider him in relation to his society, then, the society in its chronological limits at least is roughly the same as that to which Thomson's work is related. But in turning to Rossetti, one must call to mind features of this society in the main different from those that influenced Thomson. The breakdown of traditional belief, the passing of the Chartist insurgency, the conservatism of the mid-Victorian decades preceding the new ferment of the eighties, the misconceived social idealism of the Secularist movement—these are the features of the age which contribute to an understanding of Thomson's bleak though magnificent despair. Rossetti was influenced by the breakdown of belief as decisively as Thomson was, though in a different way, but apart from this one feature, it is other characteristics of the age that require attention as one turns to Rossetti's work.

Of the young Rossetti who at twenty founded the Pre-Raphaelite Brotherhood, one gets an impression of confident genius and fabulous promise. The abundant records which remain give us many glimpses of him as he exults in his joyous command of a prodigious creative impulse. Consider, for example, a letter Rossetti sent home from Paris, where he had gone on a trip with Holman Hunt in 1849. After acknowledging that the arrival of a new poem by his brother was "about the best thing that has happened since my arrival here," he copies a sonnet that "came into [his] head" while he was climbing a staircase in Notre Dame Cathedral. He goes on to tell how at the Place de la Bastille "Hunt and Broadie smoked their cigars, while I, in a fine frenzy conjured up by association and historical knowledge, leaned against the Column of July, and composed the following sonnet." After transcribing the sonnet, he comments with humorous contempt on the pictures—"mostly slosh"—in the Louvre. "The other day," he continues, "pondering on the rate of locomotion which the style of the old masters induces in us at the Louvre, I scribbled as follows—" and he transcribes another sonnet, of which three lines are:

> Meanwhile Hunt and myself race at full speed
> Along the Louvre, and yawn from school to school,
> Wishing worn-out those masters known as old.

He admits, however, that they did find some fine things in the Louvre—a fine head by Raphael "and a pastoral—at least, a kind of pastoral—by Giorgione, which is so intensely fine that I condescended to sit down before it and write a sonnet"; and once again Rossetti copies the poem for his brother. "Last night we went to Valentino's to see the cancan," he continues in the same letter. "As the groups whirled past us, one after another, in an ecstasy of sound and emotion, I became possessed with a tender rapture and recorded it in rhyme as follows. . . ."[1] Here we catch Rossetti at a moment of delighted discovery that everything he sees provides an occasion for enraptured improvisation; it is the moment of a young man's discovery of his powers.

The young members of the Brotherhood, who in an off-hand way had done nothing less than set up a new school of painting and poetry, were full of brash self-confidence. They reversed academic judgments with confident assurance and set up their own private list of great men. "Hunt and I," Rossetti tells his brother, "have prepared a list of Immortals, forming our creed, and to be pasted up in our study for the affixing of all decent fellows' signatures. It has already caused considerable horror among our acquaintance.... The list contains four distinct classes of Immortality; in the first of which three stars are attached to each name, in the second, two, in the third, one, and in the fourth, none. The first class consists only of Jesus Christ and Shakespeare."[2] They used the term "slosh" for painting in the academic style against which they were revolting, and Sir Joshua Reynolds was quickly transformed into Sir Sloshua Reynolds.[3] One is impressed constantly by their high spirits and adolescent abandon. "*Apropos* of death," Rossetti writes, "Hunt and I are going to set up among our acquaintance a Mutual Suicide Association, by the regulations whereof any member, being weary of life, may call at any time upon another to cut his throat for him. It is all of course to be done very quietly, without weeping or gnashing of teeth. I, for instance, am to go in and say, 'I say, Hunt, just stop painting that head a minute, and cut my throat'; to which he will respond by telling the model to keep the position as he shall only be a moment, and having done his duty, will proceed with the painting."[4]

Rossetti retained his high spirits, humor, and vitality throughout his twenties. The "jovial campaign," in which the Pre-Raphaelites—William Morris and Burne-Jones now added to their number—set out under Rossetti's leadership to decorate the walls of the Oxford Union building, provides many illustrations of these qualities in him. He would instigate his friends, for example, to paint fat little figures of William Morris among the sunflowers Morris was painting on the ceiling. Once he declared that Morris "would never get Iseult's head right until he had taken 'stunner Lipscombe' for his model," and sent him off to sketch the inn-keeper's beautiful daughter. "But the 'stunner's' mother, already irritated by the attention her eighteen-year-old daughter's good looks attracted from undergraduates and artists, sent Morris back crestfallen." On his return he found tacked to his bedroom door a placard announcing,

> Poor Topsy has gone
> To make a sketch of Miss Lipscombe,
> But he can't draw the head,
> And don't know where the hips come.[5]

One judges that the Artists' Rifles, formed in 1859 when there were fears of invasion from France, was an occasion for the same easy and carefree camaraderie as had marked the jovial campaign. Hunt, Morris, Burne-Jones, Millais and Swinburne all joined the Artists' Rifles along with Rossetti; Ruskin was made an honorary member. It is reported that while Morris always turned left when given the command to turn right, Rossetti was in the habit of responding to the command to form columns of fours with the question "Why?"[6] Rossetti retained something of his youthful exuberance and vitality later when he shared a house in Cheyne Walk with Swinburne, Howell, and his private menagerie of "owls, rabbits, dormice, hedgehogs, a woodchuck, a marmot, wallabies, a deer, armadillos, a raccoon, a raven, a parrot, chameleons, lizards, salamanders, a laughing jackass, a zebu, a succession of wombats"[7]—not to speak of the Brahmin bull cherished, Rossetti explained, because it had eyes like Jane Morris. When asked at this time where he got such wonderful models, he replied that on a day too dark for painting he would stand at the window and watch the passers-by: "If a lovely creature passed, I used to rush out and say, 'I'm a painter and I want to paint you.' Sometimes they would scream, then I would rush in and slam the front door."[8]

During his twenties Rossetti had such unbounded confidence in himself as to dominate all who came into his orbit, and he appears almost always to have exercised the kind of influence that awakens in others consciousness of their own worth. "For him, at that time," Mackail says, "English society was divided into two classes. The duty of the one class was to paint pictures, and it included all those who were competent to do so. The duty of the other class was to buy the pictures so painted. This amazingly simple scheme of life he enforced with all the power of his bewitching personality. To an immense power of humor and sarcasm, and a dazzling eloquence, he added gifts even more potent: an intelligence of sympathy towards the ideas or work of other artists, which Sir Edward Burne-Jones in recent years described as unequaled in his experience; a boundless generosity in helping on younger men who would be guided by him; and behind all these qualities, a certain hard intellectual force against which very few of those who came under its influence were able to make a stand."[9] "Rossetti was the planet round which we all revolved," said Val Princep; "we copied his very way of speaking. All beautiful women were 'stunners' with us. Wombats were the most delightful of God's creatures. Medievalism was our *beau idéal* and we sank our individuality in the strong personality of our adored Gabriel."[10] "He taught me," says Burne-Jones, "to have no fear or shame of my own ideas, to design perpetually, to seek no popularity, to be altogether myself—and this not in any words I can remember, but in the tenor of his conversation and in the spirit of everything he said. . . . He to me was as Pope and Emperor."[11] Ruskin recruited Rossetti to teach drawing at the Working Men's College, and there it was "a sign of Rossetti's fascinating personality," we are told, that "among these men of narrow and starved minds he was tremendously popular. Devoid of any personal concern with the general good or social improvement, he gave his best to each one. Ruskin said he was like Cimabue because he taught all he knew. It did not seem in the least abnormal to him that an artisan should want to be an artist, as he considered it the natural state of all men."[12]

Rossetti's creative vitality developed in a special direction, to understand which we must consider the character of his response to contemporary society. We should call to mind, first, certain features of the age discussed in the chapters on Carlyle, Ruskin, and Arnold. This was a society in which—not because of the iniquitous teachings of the economists, as Ruskin thought, but because of the pressures of a rapidly expanding industrialism—the business of getting and spending was laying waste man's powers in a way that even Wordsworth could not have foreseen. Acquisitive enterprise as we know it today was now for the first time establishing itself as the shaping force of society. The self-made men of the time were characterized by initiative, enterprise, driving force, frugality, self-control, and a gift for making money, but their detractors, as G. D. H. Cole reminds us, saw these virtues in a different light, painting a picture "in which initiative and enterprise were metamorphosed into greed and over-reaching, personal driving force into lust for irresponsible power, abstinence and frugality into meanness, avarice and a will to impose privation upon others, and self-control into a soulless lack of cultural values which left the new capitalists with no other interest in life than pursuit of wealth in this world and of salvation in a next world conceived in the image of their own spiritual poverty."[13] There was now emerging the society in which, as Norman Douglas puts it, men "wear away their faculties in a degrading effort to plunder one another,"[14] the society Shaw described as one of "commercialized cads . . . doing everything and anything for money, and selling [their] souls and bodies by the pound and inch after wasting half the day haggling over the price."[15]

For an understanding of Rossetti's response to his age, however, the respectability, propriety, and moral strictness of Victorian society require even greater stress than its acquisitive patterns of conduct. We can understand the force of moral conformity in the mid-nineteenth century only if we remind ourselves that the motivating force behind it lay in the consciousness of the human wrongs for which the new order was accountable. Few men, for instance, could escape at least a suspicion that Ruskin was right when he contrasted the new predatory morality with Christian ethics. The human exploitation, in England and in the colonial countries, on which the social fabric was based, was a subject concerning which most Victorians agreed to keep silent; there were certain truths, they felt, that must not be talked about. Sydney Smith told a clergyman who wanted to write a true account of what he had witnessed at the Peterloo Massacre: "A true and candid narrative of what you saw would for ever put an end to your chances of preferment."[16] If it was true in Smith's time, it was even more true later that there were certain things about contemporary civilization that could not be said. During Smith's life one could still speak with candor about the empire. It was preposterous, Smith said, for the British to take the Bible to the Indians and tell them of our ethical principle, "Thou shalt not steal": "We who, in fifty years, have extended our empire from a few acres about Madras, over the whole peninsula, and sixty millions of people, and exemplified in our public conduct every crime of which human nature is capable. What matchless impudence to follow up such practice with such precepts! If we have common prudence, let us keep the gospel at home, and tell them that Machiavelli is our prophet, and the god of the Manicheans our god."[17] But later in the century such candor became rare; except for a few men like John Morley and William Morris, those who talked about England's imperial expansion agreed not to mention the plunder but to speak instead about England's "civilizing power." Yet few men could escape at least a partial awareness of what was going on. We must look to this sense, whether conscious or unconscious, of the violations of human integrity attendant upon capitalist expansion for an explanation of the new stress on moral propriety in the

Victorian period. By placing exaggerated emphasis on rectitude in generally somewhat subsidiary matters of moral conduct the Victorians compensated for their neglect of evils they felt unable to correct, and reassured themselves about the rightness of the existing order.

It is true that the human wrongs growing out of the Victorian social system were not invariably greater than those of earlier periods; in some respects, in consequence of the humanitarian movement, they were less. But in a period when the increase in productive capacity had for the first time in history demonstrated that man has it in his power to furnish a sufficiency of the means of existence for all, it was no longer possible, as it had been earlier, to view the human costs of the established system simply as part of the eternal order of nature. Forms of exploitation previously regarded as inevitable now appeared for the first time eradicable. But they were not eradicated, and they became the subject therefore for feelings of guilt. The new governing class, one should also recall, had none of the hereditary sanctions that had enabled the aristocracy to blind itself to the human costs of the existing order. So it was that the Victorians experienced a need that was without precedent to moralize their own lives and their own society. Out of "unavowed but torturing doubts as to the validity and sanction of an enthroned bourgeoisie," Michael Sadleir says, Victorian respectability was born.[18] Hugh Kingsmill makes the same point when he says: "In Victorian England, with its fabulous increase in population and wealth, the prevailing mood was a mixture of complacency and fear. The surface was so prosperous that the dread of what lay underneath developed into an obsession which produced the extraordinary taboos that paralyzed the literature of that age."[19] To allay their fear "of what lay beneath," Kingsmill says, the Victorians mounted two sentries over their money-bags, "Sanctity-of-the-Home and Belief-in-a-Future-Life."[20]

The Victorians spent more time on "religious services, missionary meetings, and Evangelical demonstrations on controversial questions" than one would suppose they could spare from the countinghouse. They approached moral questions with a graver interest than had perhaps ever been displayed before—except by the Puritans of the seventeenth century. They employed the "herd instinct which makes men abhor all departures from custom"[21] to secure moral conformity. They developed a "curious blend of public virtue and private license," *la pudibonderie anglaise,* a new Victorian form of an age-old form of hypocrisy, which was "to become the affliction of their grandchildren and the mockery of foreign nations."[22] Perhaps the distinctive form of Victorian hypocrisy, however, was the use of moral propriety as a mask for avarice and plunder.[23] The modern hypocrite, said Belfort Bax, does not drink or chase women; he is the bishop who has shares in gold and supports wars fought in their interest.[24] The great vice of the age, in the words of Morris, was "the use of . . . cant to evade the responsibility of vicarious ferocity."[25] To many it seemed in consequence that hypocrisy had become the dominant characteristic of a society that Carlyle had described as "drenched in cant—cant religious, cant political, cant moral, cant artistic . . ."[26] "The more such a society oppresses the mass of people," Joseph Freeman says, "the louder is its talk of democracy; the more frequent and sanguinary its wars, the more it talks of peace; the greater the poverty of its wage slaves, the more it prattles about universal prosperity, and the more corrupt its sex life, the more coyly it lisps about virtue."[27] In response to such conditions the earliest anticipations now begin to manifest themselves of the somewhat general twentieth-century view that we must reconcile ourselves with the fact of "the bankruptcy, the proven fatuity, of everything that is bound up under the name of Western civilization."[28]

To the fairly large number of Victorians who responded to the new order of society with a shudder, the force of the prevailing mores appeared irresistible. It seemed that every instrumentality society possessed was being used to contribute to the pressure with which the new values were imposed. Parliament, for example, was described by Morris as "on the one side a kind of watch-committee sitting to see that the interests of the Upper Classes took no hurt, and on the other side a sort of blind to delude the people into supposing that they had some share in the management of their own affairs."[29] The constitution, described by Cobden as "a thing of monopolies, and Church-craft, and sinecures, armorial hocus-pocus, primogeniture, and pageantry,"[30] brought to the support of the current system of values the moral force of august appearances. The intellectuals, described by Morris as "the priesthood of the mumbo-jumbo of modern civilization," supplied the established order with theoretical sanctions. The intellectuals, Morris said, were "on the wrong side on almost every question that affects the right understanding of life. . . . Were I had up for any sort of crime touching property or political freedom, I should prefer to take my chance with a jury of dukes and sporting squires, rather than one of professors and college dons."[31] As for the newspapers, no censorship was required to induce them to make their contribution to the moral whitewash covering the rapacity of the established order. "Vell," H. M. Hyndman quotes a German as replying to the boast that the English did not muzzle their press, "I never did hear of no man as vas such a fool as to muzzle a sheep."[32]

Victorian prudery is to be accounted for in the main as one of the by-products of society's effort to moralize itself. This was the time when "the conspiracy to convict creation of indecency"[33] achieved its most extreme effects. It was the time when Hardy was told by his editor "that it would be more decorous and suitable for the pages of a periodical intended for family reading if the damsels" in *Tess of the D'Urbervilles* "were wheeled across the lane in a wheelbarrow" rather than carried in Angel Clare's arms, and when Hardy dutifully complied with the suggestion and rewrote the offending passage.[34] It was the time when Christina Rossetti pasted strips of paper over indelicate lines in her copy of *Atalanta in Calydon*;[35] when "a baby was not respectable until it was born"[36]—and even then there was "something vaguely 'not nice' about being a little boy";[37] when a lady is said to have remarked that "all might be well if we could have three generations of single women."[38] The story of the etiquette book of 1863 that prescribed that books by male and female authors should be kept on separate shelves—unless, that is, the authors were married—is associated with Boston, Massachusetts, not Boston, England; but it will do as well as any to suggest the lengths to which Victorian prudery could be carried. Such stories, whether aprocryphal or not, testify of course not to purity but to a morbidly intensified preoccupation with sex. "The woman who draped the legs of her piano, far from concealing her conscious and unconscious exhibitionism, ended by sexualizing the piano; no mean feat."[39] "Decency," said Shaw, is "Indecency's Conspiracy of Silence."[40] Today the main interest in stories of Victorian prudery, apart from the now somewhat outworn humor associated with them, lies in the graphic examples they supply of a dishonesty having deep roots in the social order.

The estheticism of the seventies, eighties, and nineties is best understood, then, as a response to a civilization that to many appeared so drab and dishonest that they saw no alternative except to escape from it and look elsewhere for patterns of meaning, beauty, and passion. When Burne-Jones spoke of "the perfect hunger for romance that was spread abroad in the world at the time when he came into it,"[41] he marked the beginning of the esthetic reaction against "an order of society and standard of values" that were "incapable of awakening any sort of esthetic response at all."[42] The esthetic movement, a recent critic has said, is to be viewed as a retreat from "the dominant bourgeois consciousness of the time"—a consciousness "unimaginative, petty, prosaic, 'philistine,' and hostile to art. The sensitive artist could not create in harmony with such a consciousness, and so he withdrew from the actualities about him. He renounced the bourgeois standards of morality and success and lived in dedication to his art alone."[43]

The artist withdrew from the practical concerns of his time somewhat earlier in France than in England. As early as 1835 Théophile Gautier struck out with his splendid diatribe against "useful" art:

> No, fools, no, goitrous cretins that you are, a book does not make a gelatin soup; a novel is not a pair of seamless boots; a sonnet, a syringe with a continuous jet; or a drama, a railway—all things which are essentially civilizing and adapted to advance humanity on its path of progress.
> By the guts of all the popes past, present, and future, no, and two hundred thousand times no!
> We cannot make a cotton cap out of a metonymy, or put on a comparison like a slipper; we cannot use an antithesis as an umbrella, and we cannot, unfortunately, lay a medley of rhymes on our body after the fashion of a waistcoat.[44]

In France this view of the divorce between art and practical life was further developed by Baudelaire, Verlaine, and Rimbaud. The poet, according to Verlaine, "must participate in no earthly passion, nor mingle in the commonplace doings of other men. He does not share their griefs, and should abstain from their joys. Their quarrels, their wars, the pride of republics, the arrogance of monarchies, military glory, industrial power, the prodigious expansion of science, commercial expansion, the common weal, instruction within reach of all athirst for knowledge, the amelioration of labor, the diminishing of social wretchedness, and individual suffering—all these things, which go to make up the democratic and civilizing work of society—should leave him unmoved. Dream must not take part in action."[45] So it was that in France the poets took "one road, the public another, with contempt on both sides. They mutually turned their backs, affecting not only remoteness but ignorance of the other's existence. Thus the public became more and more estranged from the poetical movement, and the poets appeared to have no place, interest, nor utility in modern society."[46] On the leaders of English estheticism who followed Rossetti—on Swinburne, Pater, Whistler, and Wilde—the influence of Gautier, Baudelaire, and Verlaine is unmistakable. Yet even so, English estheticism is not to be understood as a product of French influence but rather as a similar response to similar conditions. And in Rossetti, the initiator and in many ways most typical representative of English estheticism, the French influence was hardly discernible at all.

Nor was Rossetti's estheticism as programmatic as that of Gautier or Verlaine, or Pater or Wilde. The tenets of the Pre-Raphaelite Brotherhood had to do with artistic technique rather than with the relationship between art and society. In a number of poems—"On the Refusal of Aid between Nations," "Jenny," and "The Burden of Nineveh," for example —Rossetti deliberately comments on contemporary society. He even went so far as to offer apologies when speaking to Hall Caine about how little he had been concerned with the practical issues of life: "I judge you cannot suspect *me* of thinking the apotheosis of the early Italian poets . . . of more importance than the 'unity of a great nation.' But it is in my minute power to deal successfully (I feel) with the one, while no such entity, as I am, can advance or retard the other; and thus mine must needs be the poorer part."[47] To be sure, one feels that Rossetti is not always quite himself in his talks with Hall Caine, partly perhaps because of the disparity in age, partly because of Rossetti's failing health; one doubts that he would have talked this way earlier, or even in the later period if he had been conversing with a man to whom he cared to give a frank account of his personal feelings. It is nevertheless true that Rossetti's estheticism was not, like that of Pater and Wilde, a deliberately articulated philosophy.

From the outset of his career, however, Rossetti took it as

an assumption too obvious to require proof that only art had any real imprtance. "The dominant interest of existence, not only of his own, but of existence *per se*," W. J. Stillman said, was art, "and he tolerated nothing that sacrificed it to material or purely intellectual subjects. The artist was to him the ultimate ratio of humanity."[48] For the materials of art Rossetti went characteristically not to his own time but to the remote past—to Dante, or Malory, or esthetic-ascetic Catholicism—or to a private dream. Nor did he seek here symbols through which to express contemporary experience, as had Keats and Tennyson, his predecessors; he sought rather materials through which to create artificial effects of beauty detached from the concerns of the present. His disciples learned "within the theatre of his imagination," Doughty says, "to love, like Rossetti himself, a beauty remote from that of life and action, saddened with unreal sorrows, swept by passions existing for themselves alone, decorative agonies and ecstasies of the soul, yet real for them beyond any mundane reality."[49]

Rossetti took it for granted that the artist was superior to the moral claims of society—a thesis Wilde later advanced with all his force of paradox and epigram. "He used to say frankly," W. J. Stillman reports, "that artists had nothing to do with morality, and practically, but in a gentle and benevolent way, he made that the guiding principle of his conduct."[50] Once he protested against the impropriety of condemning to execution a beauty who happened also to be a murderess; when G. B. Hill "suggested the supremacy of the moral law even over feminine beauty," the young artists who had made Rossetti's views their own were scandalized and "overbore him with horrified cries of, 'Oh Hill, you would never hang a stunner!'"[51] Rossetti did not flout the straight-laced morality of the age, as Swinburne did. Though his *Poems* of 1870 scandalized some—notably Robert Buchanan, who attacked the volume in "The Fleshly School of Poetry"—to scandalize was not part of Rossetti's purpose, as it was of Swinburne's in *Poems and Ballads*. In his private life Rossetti took some pains, though not excessive ones, to keep up appearances. But at the same time he did not feel that the morality of his time had any claim upon him.

For Rossetti man's political life, likewise, hardly existed at all. "I can't say how it was that Rossetti took no interest in politics," said Morris; "but so it was. . . . The truth is he cared for nothing but individual and personal matters; chiefly of course in relation to art and literature, but he would take abundant trouble to help any one person who was in distress of mind or body; but the evils of any mass of people he couldn't bring his mind to bear upon. I suppose in short it needs a person of hopeful mind to take disinterested notice of politics, and Rossetti was certainly not hopeful."[52] If Morris sometimes neglected the individual for society—"Did you ever notice that Top never gives a penny to a beggar?" Rossetti remarked[53]—Rossetti neglected society for the individual, and the individual for art. "Surely . . . it must be painful to an American to see what is to be seen with you now," he wrote to Charles Eliot Norton when the Civil War was being fought, and then added characteristically: "This however is a matter so out of the current of my ideas that I am quite incompetent to speak of it."[54] William Michael Rossetti suggests that the fervent political discussions of Rossetti's father and his associates may have alienated Gabriel from politics, but a deeper reason for his apathy toward political questions would appear to be that revulsion from the age which expressed itself most characteristically in the doctrine of the supremacy of art.

If Rossetti felt less affinity with aristocrats than Wilde and Yeats, less affinity with the outcasts of society than Wilde, and less affinity with peasants than Yeats, he shared with both these poets their polar sentiments, reverence for the artist and contempt for the man of business. He despised the wealthy businessmen who paid very high prices for his paintings,[55] speaking of T. E. Plint, a Leeds stockbroker, "with pitying contempt,"[56] and describing F. Craven, a wealthy patron from Manchester, as "a grave and (let us say in a whisper) rather stupid enthusiast of the inarticulate business type."[57]

Rossetti's single-minded dedication to the cult of beauty enabled him to do a great deal of excellent work. If his paintings are spoiled to some degree by "prettiness" and by a literary content that detracts from their pictorial value, yet there is a fascination about them to which few can be insensitive. In the ballad Rossetti is capable of swift and vivid narrative, astonishing intensity, and splendid effects of weirdness and terror. He handles with mastery effects of rare poetic artifice, as in the combination of minute detail, Miltonic vastness, deliberate naïveté, and religious awe in "The Blessed Damozel." His sonnets are without equal in their intensity of feeling and severely controlled luxuriance. Like other artists of the esthetic movement, Rossetti took his craft seriously and strove tirelessly for technical perfection. Wilde's story of how he spent a morning revising his poems and added a comma, then worked the whole afternoon and took the comma out, points up a meticulousness that Wilde shared with the other authors of the esthetic movement, including Rossetti. Whistler gave another illustration of the same quality when he stared for half an hour at a canvas, then gave it a single touch and announced, "There, well, I think that will do for today."[58] Like Wilde and Whistler, and like Pater, Rossetti understood the importance of "stubborn and ceaseless limning and burnishing of one's style."[59] This it was that enabled him to construct his rich and beautiful tapestries of language, to combine the luxuriance of elaborated imagery, scriptural phrase, and resounding Latinisms, with compression and austerity.

Yet almost every reader feels that Rossetti's accomplishment in poetry was not commensurate with the great promise of his youth or with the immense powers he displayed in later life. "Upon posterity he makes the impression of a genius greater than anything he accomplished."[60] "The Blessed Damozel," written at eighteen, was Rossetti's *Vita Nuova*, R. D. Walker remarks, but no *Divine Comedy* followed—or anything faintly approaching it.[61] It is not merely that Rossetti wrote comparatively little poetry; since most of the time he looked upon himself as a painter who incidentally wrote poems rather than as a poet who incidentally painted pictures, the smallness in poetic output is understandable. It is rather that Rossetti's poetry lacks the fundamental importance that his genius might have led one to expect of it. When one reflects on this sense of disappointment, one is drawn to the conclusion that Rossetti failed to fulfill his promise in literature in part because he disintegrated, or at any rate failed to mature, as a person, and that this failure was a consequence of the way he isolated himself from contemporary experience.

In surveying Rossetti's life as a whole, not merely his glorious beginnings, one is impressed as much by failure and defeat as by creative opulence. In the years before he married Elizabeth Siddal, at thirty-two, we hear much of his "trance-like lethargy," emotional ambivalence, and paralysis of will.[62] A "wearied note . . . a baffled, frustrated tone . . . formed the burden of these perplexed, restless years."[63] Elizabeth Siddal died two years after the marriage, and thereafter Rossetti was never for long free from a sense of guilt occasioned by the uncertain circumstances of her death. From his forty-second year to his death twelve years later, insomnia, morbid despondency, remorse and paranoid delusions made his life a continuous torture and drove him to excessive drinking and to laudanum and chloral. In 1872 he almost succeeded in an attempt at suicide.

In the transition from a love of beauty as intense as that displayed by any other poet to the moral wreckage of the later years—the brooding over lost experience, depression, and despair—F. L. Lucas finds a moral; he speaks of the later experience as the inevitable consequence of Rossetti's attachment to the senses.[64] Evelyn Waugh attributes Rossetti's tortured sense of futility in the later years to a philosophic incompleteness for which both personal temperament and the environment were responsible. "Vain regret, waste, frustration—these, when all was summed up, the good taken with the bad, the gay hours with the grey, the accounts finally entered, added, and audited, were the stark conclusions of Rossetti's philosophy. *Vanitas vanitatum.* All he can bring from the abundant sources of a life of great richness and complexity is the ancient cry of outraged and bewildered humanity confronted with a world not of its own making."[65] In Rossetti, Waugh says, we are confronted with "the baffled and very tragic figure of an artist born into an age devoid of artistic standards; a man of the South, sensual, indolent, and richly versatile, exiled in the narrow, scrambling, specialized life of a Northern city; a mystic without a creed; a Catholic without the discipline or consolation of the Church. . . ."[66] At the same time Waugh's judgment upon Rossetti's personal inadequacies is severe: "There was fatally lacking in him that *essential rectitude* that underlies the serenity of all really great art. The sort of unhappiness that beset him was not the sort of unhappiness that does beset a great artist; all his brooding about magic and suicide are symptomatic not so much of genius as of mediocrity. There is a spiritual inadequacy, a sense of ill-organization about all that he did."[67]

It would seem clear that the wreckage of Rossetti's later life must be regarded as in part at least a consequence of his isolation from the society of his day. For it is through a meaningful relationship with society that a man typically adjusts the conflicting elements in his personality and gives pattern to his life. When Rossetti turned away from his age in order to set up his private priesthood of beauty, he deprived himself of the means through which other men come to whatever maturity they are capable of, and henceforth the varied impulses within him were left to express themselves without that principle of direction which might have brought them within a coherent framework.

Rossetti's strongest single impulse was associated with the dream of an ideal love—a dream for which the Dante-Beatrice relationship supplied the pattern. Rossetti had translated the *Vita Nuova* when in his teens, and thereafter he continually saw his life in the image of Dante's, continually searched for the twin soul, the elect, dedicated spirit, for which his nature yearned. "Unless we realize . . . the basic fact that both his life and art were dominated by dream," says Oswald Doughty, "that he was trying to live his myth, his 'one dream alone' (for him, almost the sole important reality), both his art and life must be scarcely comprehensible."[68] Rossetti found the great spiritualizing love in Elizabeth Siddal (for a time) and he found it again in Jane Morris; of this we may be sure whether or not we accept in detail Oswald Doughty's reconstruction of the relationship between Rossetti and Jane Morris. Rossetti's dream of ideal love was a young man's dream— an adolescent dream, one might almost say; it was associated with a conception of love that the mature person generally supersedes. Instead of passing from the youthful dream to the discovery of values consistent with what the real world has to offer, as he might have done had he been a part of a society in whose activities and purposes he was prepared to share, Rossetti clung desperately to the dream as his one means of giving significance and intensity to his life. No sooner had he found the ideal love with Elizabeth Siddal, however, than it began to fail him. The reality was disappointing when contrasted with the unattainable ideal, and Lizzie "no longer seemed to him 'the woman who was his soul.'" So there followed "languor," "boredom," "waning desire."[69] Though with Lizzie he no longer experienced the "mystical recognition of twin souls," yet "somewhere, he dreamed, that elect, dedicated spirit awaited him."[70] There were "quarrels and reconciliations, emotional ambivalences in which love became hate and hate love."[71] The old romance had "turned stale, lost its ecstasy, its once visionary delight, substituting problems for poetry,"[72] and life with Lizzie became enveloped in an "atmosphere of sickness, seriousness, reproach, rancor, misunderstanding, and lack of sympathy."[73]

When the ideal love was in eclipse, he gave expression to other impulses in his many-sided nature. There was the impulse, for example, that led him to the type of experience he used in "Jenny" and in "Found"; the impulse that led to his "swift and unscrupulous" amours, characterized, as Waugh puts it, by "insolence of inception, energy of enjoyment, and vagueness of termination";[74] the impulse that led him later—when he was living at Cheyne Walk with Swinburne and Howell in the sixties—to explore the "acrid putrescence" of London;[75] the impulse that later fulfilled itself in the easy-going, unrefined menage he kept up intermittently with Fanny Cornforth. Because Rossetti had isolated himself from the social attachments through which the personality achieves coherence, he neither inhibited these impulses nor found for them a mode of expression not damaging to the personality. The result was that he indulged them only to be tortured by a sense of guilt and betrayal, and was thrown back once again to a "dependence upon an ideal love to save him from his own lower nature."[76]

In telling of the contents of the note Elizabeth Siddal pinned to her dress when she took an overdose of laudanum, Helen Rossetti Angeli removes the doubt that has always existed as to whether or not Lizzie committed suicide.[77] But while we know that she took her life deliberately, what Rossetti's responsibility was will never be known. There were rumors that his repeated infidelities had driven her to construe each absence as a betrayal, that on the night of Lizzie's death he had been out with another woman.[78] Whatever his culpability may have been, it is clear that guilt associated with Lizzie's death was a main component of the torture of the later years. "All the evidence . . . suggests it was this uncertainty about his wife's death, along with other disappointments and uncertainties of Gabriel's later life, acting upon so 'anxious' and unstable a temperament as his, that ultimately led him, by the path of mental, moral and emotional decay, to attempt suicide by means of the very drug which had destroyed his wife."[79]

Whether Jane Morris had superseded Elizabeth Siddal as the ideal love before Rossetti's marriage we cannot know, but it appears likely. Rossetti, not Morris, had discovered Jane Burden during the "Jovial Campaign," attracted as he was by her "dark, passionate, un-English beauty."[80] Rumor had it that he fell in love with her at once. Jane's beauty surpassed even that of Elizabeth Siddal. "To think of Morris's having that wonderful and most perfect stunner of his to look at or even speak to," Swinburne exclaimed. "The idea of his marrying her is insane. To kiss her feet is the utmost men should dream of doing."[81] Jane Morris was the beauty about whom Graham Robertson said, "I always recommended would-be but wavering worshippers to start with Mrs. Stillman (Marie Spartali) who was, so to speak, Mrs. Morris for Beginners. The two marvels had many points in common: the same lofty stature, the same long sweep of limb, the 'neck like a tower,' the night-dark tresses and the eyes of mystery, yet Mrs. Stillman's loveliness conformed to the standard of ancient Greece and could at once be appreciated, while study of her trained the eye to understand the more esoteric beauty of Mrs. Morris and 'trace in Venus' eyes the gaze of Proserpine.' "[82] Whatever Rossetti's relations with Jane Morris may have been in the earlier years, Oswald Doughty makes it clear that his love for Jane was the main source of his poetic renaissance at about the age of forty, and that she, not Elizabeth Siddal, was the inspiration of most of the sonnets of "The House of Life"—a point on which both Rossetti and his brother sought to mislead.[83] Though Rossetti was now in middle life, his love for Jane remained the youthful dream of "The Blessed Damozel," the kind of love that in the nature of things can never be fulfilled. Meanwhile there continued the "adventures of promiscuity and of grotesque encounter" which Rossetti relished,[84] and which satisfied a part of his nature but only a part, and at the cost of guilt and remorse; and there continued, too, the relationship with Fanny Cornforth, housekeeper and mistress, "vulgar, vital, primitive, the antithesis of the over-strained ideal of 'The Blessed Damozel.' "[85] Fanny was "the simplest, the most real of all the women Gabriel knew; she asked no romantic sentiment, no heroics."[86] But between Rossetti and Fanny Cornforth there was a minimum of intellectual affinity; he was embarrassed by a certain vulgarity in her speech; when his friends were present he tried to keep her out of the way.

In his relationships with women Rossetti was far from the norms of conventional morality, but that is not the point that needs to be stressed; one may grant a measure of justice to Rossetti's view that the artist should not subject himself to the constraints of ordinary morality. What needs to be stressed is Rossetti's failure to outgrow a youthful conception of love and his failure to integrate the varying impulses of his nature, to make them subserve a creative end. In his attempt to unite body and soul, to be sure, to establish a oneness between sense and spirit, a powerful integrating impulse was at work; and this theme is the source of the enduring value of many of the "House of Life" sonnets. But apart from this one effort to achieve unification, the conflicting tendencies of Rossetti's nature warred with one another with the most destructive results.

Rossetti's failure to unify his own nature is reflected also in matters of belief. At heart he was a pagan and skeptic, like Morris, but at the same time he was attracted by "the blessed mutter of the mass," by the ritual and mystery of medieval Christianity. Too much the skeptic to take seriously the religious sentiment he used for poetic purposes, he was at the same time too much attached to this sentiment to endure the chaffing of a disbeliever like William Bell Scott.[87] He had a strong interest, acquired from his father perhaps, in all forms of the occult, for magic, symbolism, mystic initials and numbers. Had he formed his nature through the agency of social relationships he would certainly have outgrown this interest, but instead he indulged it and even took up spiritualism for a time after his wife's death.[88] Throughout his life, too, he indulged obsessional interests that would have been brought under control had he achieved maturity; love and guilt,[89] love and death,[90] the fallen woman are examples of obsessional themes in Rossetti's work. The same failure in integration which allowed him to surrender to these obsessional interests left him a prey during the last ten years of his life to "the belief in a secret conspiracy against himself," the paranoid "fear of lurking treachery."[91] He was "devoured by that distressing and not uncommon delusion that the whole world was banded together against him in a conspiracy of infinite ramifications."[92] He discovered an attack on himself in Browning's "Fifine at the Fair" and was sure Lewis Carroll was satirizing him in "The Hunting of the Snark." "Malevolence stared at him in the eyes of strangers in the street; every tiny mishap in his everyday life—a tube of paint mislaid, a plate cracked—had become in his mind the work of his enemies."[93] When Robert Buchanan attacked him in "The Fleshly School of Poetry," it seemed to Rossetti "as if the whole power of society had descended on him in retribution."[94]

It does not help to dismiss the problem here by saying that Rossetti belongs to a psychoneurotic type. To be sure, the obsessions and the paranoia are neurotic symptoms. Rossetti conforms almost precisely, as a matter of fact, to an abnormal personality type described by Frances Wickes in *The Inner World of Man*—the type of the artist preoccupied with the *anima* and dedicated to the creation of beauty at the sacrifice of his personal relationships.[95] But neurotic potentialities as great as those apparent in the young Rossetti exist in almost every normal person. At twenty, as we have seen, Rossetti appears to have been a singularly confident and healthy individual. To explain the morbid development of neurotic tendencies in Rossetti one must take into account not merely the personality type itself but also the way his failure to relate to society deprived him of the instrument through which he might have formed his own nature. "One thing is very certain," Ruskin once wrote to Elizabeth Siddal, "that Rossetti will never be happy or truly powerful till he gets over that habit of his of doing nothing but what 'interests him'—and you also must try and read the books I am going to send you, which you know are to be chosen from among the most *un*interesting I can find."[96] And again—this time in the petulant, maiden-aunt manner he sometimes assumed—Ruskin wrote to Rossetti: "If you wanted to oblige *me,* you would keep your room in order, and go to bed at night. All your fine speeches go for nothing with me till you do that."[97] Knowing Ruskin's command of language, we may be sure that when he said this he was saying something literal and at the same time using a symbol. Rossetti did not keep his room in order—that is the source of his failure to fulfill the promise of his beginnings.

Matthew Arnold, as the poems show, had as strong a tendency toward psychoneurotic development as Rossetti, but he did what Rossetti failed to do; he related himself to people and to the age in such a way as to give a coherent structure to his own personality. Not that this adjustment eliminated all conflicts; some, as a matter of fact, it intensified, as was shown in the Arnold chapter, but these were not conflicts of the kind that lead to personal disorganization. Much of the work of Carlyle, Ruskin, and James Thomson is rightly to be understood in terms of psychoneurotic tendencies, for though each of them made the effort that is lacking in Rossetti to find his relationship to the age, the relationship was distorted to a greater or less degree in each instance by inner compulsions beyond the individual's control. In Rossetti, on the other hand, neurotic tendencies not greater than exist in most normal persons were permitted to develop unchecked because of the poet's failure to relate himself to his society. It would be as misleading to explain Rossetti's abnormality merely in terms of neurotic causes, forgetting his unsatisfactory relationship to his age, as to explain Thomson's abnormality merely in terms of his relationship to his age, forgetting the neurotic causes. Rossetti's tragedy lies in the nineteenth-century breakdown in communication between the individual and society; it is only by reference to that phenomenon that one can understand why he was forever returning to "his own unfathomable and incommunicable despair."[98]

For posterity Rossetti's tragedy is literary, not personal; it lies not in the disproportionate share of suffering that was the lot of this enormously gifted man but in the fact that his literary work lacks the first-rate importance of which initially he was capable. For all his great gift of expression, his command of elaborate, grave, and rich rhythms, his austere control of luxurious imagery, Rossetti's work does not sustain us like that of the great poets. It is "of the esoteric order," as Pater said.[99] Emerson was right when he said that Rossetti's work was not of the highest significance but something "exotic."[100] When he treats the theme of sense and spirit and the mystic role of woman as the "logos" that unites the two, Rossetti speaks directly and persuasively on a subject of major importance. But in the theme of love and death and guilt, in his factitious constructs of asceticism and awe, in the erotic idealism of the worship of beauty, Rossetti is expressing, one feels, an imperfectly formed nature and "trying to bring into line the mature passions of manhood with the idealism of youth."[101] We read him because we become absorbed in the rarefied and curious private experience rather than because he touches forcefully upon the universals of human experience. "It seems a pity," Stopford Brooke says justly, though with a touch of Victorian moralizing, "that so much good poetry, subtle feeling, careful thought and art should be expended on a kind of love which, however varied its phases, is, when it is made the sole interest of life, so fleeting, so isolating. It is natural, even needful, to pass through its house in youth, but men and women have other and fairer houses to dwell in permanently. All the greater poets have felt this. They have written lyrics of this great passion, but these are only incidental. Their real work is elsewhere in humanity."[102]

In his use of the preternatural one feels that Rossetti is indulging a private, and in the last analysis frivolous, interest in strange and forbidden things, rather than, like Coleridge or Kafka, discovering fresh symbols for general human experience. Even Rossetti's language—his triumph—has about it a preciousness that cannot be dissociated from the tenuousness and remoteness of his subject matter. His work is that of the "goldsmith," as Elton says, or of "the Indian who inlays marble flower petals into the marble tomb of an emperor." He rejoices in "the sorting of colored words, in bevelling the sentences, in blowing away the dust. It is the joy of decoration, which insensibly carries [him] away from natural forms into strangeness."[103] Rossetti's poetry, in short, is a curiosity in literature. Only those who relate themselves in more significant ways than he did to the affairs of men are able to do work of fundamental literary importance. Modern artists who have done the best work, Christopher Caudwell says, have discovered that they "cannot be content," as Rossetti was, "to be 'pure artists,' but must also be prophets, thinkers, philosophers, and politicians, men interested in life and social reality as a whole."[104]

Given the bias of his temperament and the state of Victorian society as described at the beginning of this chapter, it was perhaps almost inevitable that Rossetti should have developed as he did. If the foregoing pages have implied a censorious attitude toward Rossetti, that is merely an unfortunate by-product of the necessities of exposition; no attitude could be more ridiculous than one of fault-finding in dealing with experience of this type. Rossetti must be seen, rather, as the tragic symbol of an age in which the artist faced unprecedented and, for many, insuperable difficulties in relating himself to his fellow men and in bringing his individuality to maturity as one can do only through the agency of such relationships.

Seven

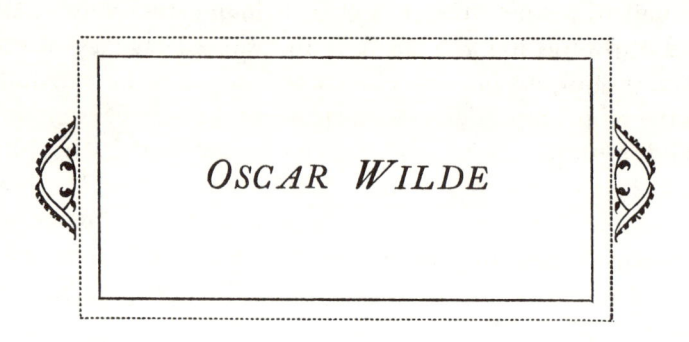

OSCAR WILDE

IN OSCAR WILDE MANIFEST WEAKNESSES WERE COMBINED WITH extraordinary gifts. The weaknesses were those of the poseur—the esthete with loose collar, flowing green tie, and knee breeches, perpetually *mot*ing so that others might reap (to quote one of Wilde's puns). Samuel Chew's charge of "fundamental insincerity"[1] in Wilde is too strong, but no one who enjoyed playing to the gallery as he did could be sincere for any long stretch of time. "The dog on his hind legs is . . . humanity," said George Moore, and Wilde would have agreed; "we are all on our hind legs striving to astonish somebody, and that is why I honor respectability; if there were nobody to shock, our trade would come to an end, and for this reason I am secretly in favor of all the cardinal virtues."[2] Wilde's best gifts were displayed when he employed wit, paradox, and epigram, and a deft control of the comedy of manners, to astonish and shock.

What is equally important and less apparent, however, is that along with William Morris and George Bernard Shaw, Wilde was one of the first to express a new time spirit, that like these authors he possessed the uncommon gift of ethical creativity. Shaw says that a physician once told him he had "normal" eyesight—that is, like some ten per cent of the people, he saw things accurately. Shaw goes on to say that perhaps the same thing was true of his moral vision: "All I had to do was to open my normal eye, and with my utmost literary skill put the case exactly as I saw it, to be applauded as the most humorously extravagant paradoxer in London."[3] Wilde's paradoxes are also marked by the quality that Shaw described as "normal vision." Wilde measures up to Shaw's definition of a genius as "a person who, seeing farther and probing deeper than other people, has a different set of ethical valuations from theirs, and has energy enough to give effect to this extra vision and its valuations in whatever manner best suits his or her specific talents."[4]

Wilde, G. J. Renier says, has been "fantastically underestimated" by the English. "They have been blinded by the pose of his earlier years, and by revelations concerning his personal life which were made at the time of his trial in 1895. They seem unable to regard him otherwise than as a *poseur* or a degenerate."[5] It has been easy to see the qualities of flamboyancy and verve Wilde shares with Shaw, but less easy to see the ethical creativity that he shared with him also, or to see that Wilde, like Shaw, was "in the forefront of a revolution in morals."[6] At least one astute contemporary, however, gave it as his view that Wilde had not only "more wit" but "a much deeper view of life than his follower, Bernard Shaw,"[7] and this estimate is as near the truth as the conventional one.

In seeking the clue to Wilde's originality we must look partly to his own gifts and partly to the times, for here, as in every significant contribution to culture, qualities of the man and the moment propitiously combine. Some traits in Wilde's personality produced effects in his literary work quite as dubious as their effects in his personal life. The cult of sin in Wilde, for example, produced literary manifestations invariably tainted with a puerility that embarrasses the reader. It had its source in a fad of the decadence, and also, one supposes, in some repression that gave a morbid fascination to forbidden experience. Wilde often gave evidence, too, of an impulse toward self-punishment similar in kind to the impulse that was powerfully developed in James Thomson, though less strong. Like Rossetti, he enacted his tragedy many times before it happened;[8] at the time of the trial, there is no question that he to some extent purposely brought about his own destruction by abandoning discretion in his testimony and rejecting the chances that were given him to escape. The secret desire for catastrophe that has been said to exist in every man was abnormally developed in Wilde, and its literary results—in "Pen, Pencil and Poison," for example—are no more satisfactory than those associated with Rossetti's obsessional interests.

The trait that contributed most to Wilde's originality was his confidence in the spontaneous side of his own nature. The free, expansive forces of the personality had great strength in Wilde; inhibition and restraint were less rigorous in him than in most men. Yeats said that Wilde lived in the enjoyment of his own spontaneity.[9] His confidence in the spontaneous self, like the impulse toward self-destruction and the cult of sin, contributed no doubt to the debacle of his life, but at the same time it freed him from that distrust of human potentialities that in men like Carlyle and Ruskin, and to a lesser extent Arnold, is associated with a distrust of one's own spontaneous nature. Wilde possessed also a degree of insight into the more obscure mechanisms of the personality that in a pre-Freudian must strike one as remarkable. "It is the passions about whose origin we deceive ourselves," he says, anticipating one aspect of Freudian psychology, "that tyrannize most strongly over us."[10] When he says that "the mutilation of the savage has its tragic survival in the self-denial that mars our lives,"[11] he shows that he has the psychiatrist's understanding of how primitive modes of experience survive in the unconscious. No one, again, could better phrase the morbid consequences of repression than to say, as Wilde did, that the soul "grows sick with longing for the things it has forbidden itself, with desire for what its monstrous laws have made monstrous and unlawful."[12] There can be little question that the grasp of the hidden ways of the soul manifested in remarks like these did much to make it possible for Wilde to go beyond the conventional thinking of his day.

To make clear the way the social climate contributed to Wilde's originality we must remind ourselves of the degree to which, in the eighties and nineties, confidence in the established order was shaken, and of the growth in those decades of new attitudes toward social change. The ideological ferment of the eighties grew out of economic crisis and depression, much as did the ferment of the nineteen-thirties in the United States; Helen Lynd[13] and others have commented on the likenesses between these decades in the two countries. In 1874 there began a long period of wage reductions, unemployment, and industrial depression,[14] accompanied by strikes and mass demonstrations such as the march of the unemployed that led to the "Bloody Sunday" rioting of November 13, 1887. At the same time the Secularist and republican movements of the eighteen-seventies with which Thomson had been associated gave way to the spectacular rise of socialism in the eighties. Mill, Darwin, Spencer, Huxley, Malthus, and Ingersoll, as Shaw reminds us, were superseded by Henry George and Karl Marx. Henry George's *Progress and Poverty* sold in enormous quantities in England in the eighties; Marx's theories were popularized by H. M. Hyndman in *England for All,* published in 1881. No less than four socialist parties were formed in this decade. Subjects of discussion throughout Lancashire and Yorkshire, Hyndman tells us, were John Stuart Mill's conversion to socialism, Henry George's *Progress and Poverty,* Bellamy's *Looking Backward,* Morris's *News from Nowhere,* Hyndman's own *England for All,* and Marx's *Capital* and *The*

Communist Manifesto.[15] In part this was a revival of a radicalism going back to Chartist days; some of the older men who attended Morris's lectures, for example, had been Chartists or Owenites in their youth.[16] But in the main the ferment was less the revival of an older radicalism than a response to new economic conditions.

It was not only economic breakdown that gave rise to new social perspectives; more important, perhaps, was the threat of war. England fought the Afghanistan War in 1878-79, the Zulu War in 1879, and the Boer War at the end of the century, and throughout these two decades it seemed likely that a great war with Czarist Russia might break out at any time. For the first time the assumption now became general that war is a perhaps inevitable consequence of the present form of industrialism. "It is now a desperate 'competition' between the great nations of civilization for the world-market," said Morris, "and tomorrow it may be a desperate war for that end."[17] It was not so much the economic maladjustments in England as the threat of war with Russia in 1877 that directed William Morris's thinking toward socialism.[18] In this year "The Great MacDermott" gave the language a new word with his music-hall song,

> We don't want to fight, but by Jingo if we do,
> We've got the ships, we've got the men,
> And we've got the money too . . .[19]

and henceforth jingoism remained a constantly menacing element in the national life. Jingoism had appeared before; it was manifested during the Crimean War by Tennyson in "Maud" and by Kingsley in his sermons for soldiers.[20] But the jingoism of the last two decades of the century was marked by a hysterical intensity for which there was no recent precedent and reënforced by all the frightening power of modern journalism. Hyndman speaks of the "furious chauvinism" that "seemed to have got hold of a large proportion of the people" at the time of the Boer War, when a "great Empire" was involved in a "war with a population of farming folk no bigger than that of Brighton all told."[21] "The display of hysterical and even maniacal joy and exuberance on Mafeking night in London," he says, "surpassed in unseemly indecency anything I could have imagined. The whole manifestation spoke of a people in decay."[22]

Many people soon became convinced that militaristic excitement was in part being deliberately fomented to divert attention from troubles at home. It was noted as significant that the threat of war with Russia over the "Eastern Question" beginning in 1876 coincided with the beginning of an industrial depression, and that for many years the excitement over Bulgarian atrocities dwarfed domestic issues in the press and in parliament.[23] The parliamentary session of 1879 passed no significant social legislation because of preoccupation with Afghanistan and Zululand, just as the previous session had failed to give attention to domestic problems because of the threat of war with Russia.[24] In his "Manifesto to the Working Men of England," in 1877, Morris called on the workers to resist the attempt of both major parties to divert their attention from domestic problems by rattling swords in the Near East.[25] It was felt generally, in a word, that the "Have-and-Holders," as Shaw puts it, were staving off the threat of unwelcome social change by using the device of "leading the herd to war, which immediately and infallibly makes them forget everything, even their most cherished and hard-won public liberties and private interests, in the irresistible surge of their pugnacity and the tense preoccupation of their terror."[26]

Some writers of the last two decades—Kipling and Henley, most notably—gave literary expression to the new chauvinism. Others—Pater, Wilde himself, and the writers associated with *The Yellow Book*—experiencing now all the more strongly the revulsion from the age that had impelled Rossetti toward his cult of beauty, brought English estheticism into full flower. To a greater or less degree these writers, with their "fingering of their own emotions," and preoccupation with perverse experience, manifested decadent trends in their work; they "made romance out of exhaustion and excess."[27] The most distinctive trend in the literature of the last two decades, however, was not jingoism, or estheticism, or decadence, but a new confidence in the creative potentialities of the human spirit. The authors who established this trend were Wilde, Morris, and Shaw.

These authors rejected the dominant values of the age as flatly as did Rossetti. The qualities which Wilde stressed when he spoke of the businessmen of his day, for instance, were "their heavy inaccessibility to ideas, their dull respectability, their tedious orthodoxy, their worship of vulgar success, their entire preoccupation with the gross materialistic side of life, and their ridiculous estimate of their own importance."[28] For Wilde as for Arnold, American civilization represented the apotheosis of the middle-class spirit, and the qualities he stressed when speaking of America were its "crude commercialism," its "materializing spirit," its "indifference to the poetical side of things," and its "lack of imagination and of high unattainable ideals."[29] But the response of these authors was different from Rossetti's, for if they were equally repelled by contemporary civilization, they nevertheless possessed a social faith which he lacked.

The men who responded to this new time-spirit of the eighties and nineties were in general agreed that the structure of society must be altered as a first step toward the redemption of individuals; in this respect they differed from Carlyle, Ruskin, and Arnold, all of whom considered that the individual must be changed as a first step toward the redemption of society. Tom Mann represents the new outlook when he says that 1880 marked a decisive turning point in his life "because in this year I first began to realize that the faults of individuals, and the evils of the community, the existence of which I deplored, were not to be eliminated or cured by urging individuals of every class and station to live 'godly, righteous, and sober lives.'"[30] Morris represents the new outlook when he says that he once thought that "the ugly disgraces of civilization might be got rid of by the conscious will of intelligent persons: yet as I strove to stir up people to this reform, I found that the causes of the vulgarities of civilization lay deeper than I had thought, and little by little I was driven to the conclusion that all these uglinesses are but the outward expression of the innate moral baseness into which we are forced by our present form of society, and that it is futile to attempt to deal with them from the outside."[31]

It was with this conviction that Morris returned to social questions after the years devoted to a more or less escapist art. As an undergraduate at Cambridge, Morris, along with Burne-Jones and the other undergraduates who published *The Oxford and Cambridge Magazine* in 1856, had been seriously concerned with questions of social reform. Burne-Jones had written of the "Crusade and Holy Warfare against the Age" which was part of their aim.[32] But then Morris came under the irresistible influence of Rossetti, who taught him that Malory's *Morte d'Arthur* was "the greatest book in the world"[33] and diverted his interest from social reform to art—to an art, like Rossetti's, having the most tenuous affinities with real life. Now in the late eighteen-seventies, Morris returned to social questions, and he did so with the new conviction that they must be approached by attempting not to reform individuals but to re-form society. He now understood something that Ruskin was never able to grasp, that the individuals who profit most from the existing order are generally good men, honorable and benevolent in their intentions, not at all conscious of being oppressors of the poor; "they live in an orderly, quiet way themselves," he said, "as far as possible removed from the feelings of a Roman slave-driver or a Legree."[34] It was the existing form of society, Morris now believed, that compelled such men as these to sacrifice to the end of cheap products, often not worth producing, "the happiness of the workman at his work, nay, his most elementary comfort and bare health."³⁵ His task now, as he saw it, was to help build an organization capable of transforming the structure of society itself; that is why he gave his time to committee meetings, support of the radical press, speech-making, and the thousand duties required of a man whose aim is not to preach or to teach but to organize. Many at this time agreed with the sentiment H. D. Traill expressed in "The Poet and the Police-Court," that it would be well if Morris's good genius could

> Take him from things he knoweth not the hang of,
>   Relume his fancy and snuff out his "views,"
> And in the real Paradise he sang of
>   Bid him forget the shadow he pursues.³⁶

But it was only now that Morris discovered his real powers. His writing at this time, as Shaw says, "which the most uppish of his friends regarded as a deplorable waste of the time of a great artist, really called up all his mental reserves for the first time."³⁷

Shaw himself voices the new point of view when he says it used to be believed "that you could not make men good by Act of Parliament," but "we now know that you cannot make them good in any other way." "In short," he adds, "Christianity, good or bad, right or wrong, must perforce be left out of the question in human affairs until it is made practically applicable to them by complicated political devices. . . . Personal righteousness, and the view that you cannot make people moral by Act of Parliament, is, in fact, the favorite defensive resort of people who, consciously or subconsciously, are quite determined not to have their property meddled with by Jesus or any other reformer."³⁸ When he says that a society "which desires to found itself on a high standard of integrity of character in its units should organize itself in such a fashion as to make it possible too for all men and all women to maintain themselves in reasonable comfort by their industry without selling their affections and their convictions,"[39] Shaw exhibits again the new view that the form of society must take precedence over personal morality. It may be true that the Fabian Society at times discouraged young men from "real co-operation with the mass of the workers" and led them to "discuss social problems and propound doctrinaire solutions with little or no direct reference to the actual facts of life," as Hyndman charged,[40] yet even Hyndman paid tribute to the contribution Shaw made to the building of radical organizations during the twelve years when he spoke on an average three times a week on street corners and at radical clubs.[41] It was the new outlook of the last decades of the century that enabled Shaw, as it enabled Morris, to go through that kind of ordeal.

The influence of Marxist theory was undoubtedly one cause of the shift in stress from the individual to society, but the extent of Marx's influence is hard to measure because it was often indirect. Hyndman's *England for All*, for example, is little more than a popularization of Marx, but Hyndman did not mention Marx's name in the book because he believed that hostility toward the communist theoretician was so great that to mention him would detract from the book's success.[42] Shaw speaks for many besides himself, however, when he says that "Marx was a revelation. His abstract economics, I discovered later, were wrong, but he rent the veil. He opened my eyes to the facts of history and civilization, gave me an entirely fresh conception of the universe, provided me with a purpose and a mission in life."[43]

Those who responded to the new spirit of the last decades possessed what Tom Mann said Henry George had given him, "a glorious hope for the future of humanity" and "a firm conviction that the social problem could and would be solved."[44] The quality of this new vision is seen best perhaps in Morris. His aim was to secure not only political freedom but economic emancipation also.[45] He was interested not in dividing up the wealth but in establishing a form of society that would direct human energies toward constructive ends.[46]

He was in search of a way not to destroy the machine, as Ruskin often wished to do, but to master it: "It is the allowing machines to be our masters and not our servants that so injures the beauty of life nowadays."[47] The words he spoke at the funeral of Alfred Linnell, who was killed on "Bloody Sunday," show in their simple dignity the quality of the social vision that sustained him: "Our friend who lies here has had a hard life and met with a hard death, and if society had been differently constituted, his life might have been a delightful, a beautiful and a happy one. It is our business to begin to organize for the purpose of seeing that such things shall not happen."[48] It was because their aim was to do more than satisfy economic wants that men at this time felt themselves, like Cobden and Bright earlier, to be not merely leaders of a class but "soldiers"—as Matthew Arnold would have said, employing the Heine quotation that seemed to him so expressive—in the "liberation warfare of humanity." "It is always assumed by the educated ignorant," H. M. Hyndman declared, "that Socialists limit their aspiration to the kitchen and the table, and that ill-nourished minds make a god of a full belly for their half-fed bodies. Nothing can be more absurd. No sooner does any human being grasp the truths of Socialism than his capacity for the appreciation of beauty in Nature and Art begins to grow. That I have always observed. And many a working man has told me in grim seriousness that what makes him hate the existing social system and the class which administers it so bitterly as to render him, in thought and action, a dynamiter, but for the innate consciousness that this wild justice of revenge could have no permanent effect on the social state, is that he and his have been shut out, not only from complete physical development by insufficiency of food and adequate clothing and housing, but that all the higher part of his nature has been starved and stunted by privation of any opportunity in childhood and youth for learning to love beauty for its own sake."[49]

The actual progress toward accomplishment of these goals

was so slow that Hyndman, among others, was hard put to it to find an explanation. The English workers, he concludes regretfully, lack both the fighting idealism of the French and the patience and discipline of the Germans.[50] Emigration, bad food, bad housing, and lack of education and physical exercise have deprived the nation of its most vigorous stock.[51] The English workers now, unlike those of the Chartist period, are afraid "of shocking the tender susceptibilities of the middle class";[52] he accuses them of "lack of grit"[53] and of a "systematic and degrading respect of their 'betters.' "[54] He returns to the "ignorance, apathy, physical deterioration, and the servility engendered by sheer hopelessness" in the working class.[55] Conditions are ripe for social change, he says, but the workers lack "adequate intellectual capacity."[56] Perhaps the trouble may lie in the initial mistake against which Bronterre O'Brien had warned during the Chartist period, the mistake of forming skilled trade unions "which could scarcely fail to constitute a buffer on the side of the capitalists."[57] Yet all these reasons appear to Hyndman inadequate and he acknowledges that a satisfactory explanation eludes him.[58] The "possessing classes" have not yet seen fit "to bribe, or to cajole, or to organize spies and agents of provocation systematically, or, in short, to use in earnest the many weapons of defense which lie ready to their hand";[59] they have not resorted to the strategies used by the aristocracy before the Reform Bill, because the agitation for change, as yet so much weaker than the earlier one, has not forced these strategies upon them. Despite the inexplicably slow rate of advance, however, throughout this period, those who had responded to the new time-spirit retained for the most part a steady confidence in their objectives.

There were times when Wilde responded to the new time-spirit as confidently as did Morris, or Hyndman, or Tom Mann, or Shaw; of these times "The Soul of Man under Socialism" is the best record. "It is a question whether we have ever seen the full expression of a personality, except in the imaginative plane of art," he says, but he believes that a form of society may be achieved which will make this "full expression" possible.[60] He believes there may still lie ahead a "great period of national united energy,"[61] which will make possible for the individual a greater measure of self-realization than is now attainable. "I believe that if one were to live out his life fully and completely, were to give form to every feeling, expression to every thought, reality to every dream—I believe that the world would gain such a fresh impulse of joy that we would forget the maladies of medievalism, and return to the Hellenic ideal—to something finer, richer, than the Hellenic ideal, it may be."[62] But if this is to be accomplished, Wilde says, the form of society which keeps men "wounded, or worried, or maimed, or in danger"[63] must be changed.

To be sure, this was a transient view with Wilde. After the trial, as *De Profundis* shows, he reverted to traditional modes of moral experience; we see in him then, no doubt, something of that regression following upon a traumatic experience of which Abram Kardiner writes in *The Traumatic Neurosis of War*[64] and of which Sue Brideshead of *Jude the Obscure* provides an example in fiction. But even before the trial if Wilde at times shared Morris's belief that a change in the form of society might release what he finely described as "the great actual Individualism latent and potential in mankind generally,"[65] yet his characteristic attitude had more in it of Rossetti than of Morris. "A true artist," he would then say, "takes no notice whatever of the public. The public to him is non-existent."[66] The authority of the people "is a thing blind, deaf, hideous, grotesque, tragic, amusing, serious and obscene. It is impossible for the artist to live with the People. All despots bribe. The people bribe and brutalize."[67] These two attitudes toward people vie with one another in "The Soul of Man under Socialism," but in Wilde's work as a whole there is no question that he more often showed an affinity with Rossetti than with Morris.

Nevertheless, it was the vision he at times shared with Morris and Shaw that gave a constructive slant to his most reckless paradoxes and enabled him to initiate a new ethical outlook which is still in the process of maturing today and whose emergence is the first sign of the dissolution of the Victorian synthesis. If some critics have missed Wilde's importance in this regard, the reason is perhaps that he employed paradox and epigram rather than argument, and seldom dropped the disguise of moral irresponsibility. Shaw was influenced by Wilde when he worked out his own literary formula, which was, he explained, to "think your problem out until you have got to the bottom of it, and when you have reached a point at which your solution will seem so simple that it will sound like the first notion that would come into any fool's head, deliver it with the utmost levity. Thus," Shaw argued, "you entertain your audience and score irresistibly over the parliamentary humbugs whose art it is to cover up by the most impressive gravity the fact that they are saying nothing at the greatest endurable or unendurable length."[68] Perhaps Wilde's levity has sometimes concealed the importance of what he has to say, as Shaw's has done. But it is true at the same time, as with Shaw, that the importance of what Wilde had to say contributed to the excellence of his style. "A true and original style," Shaw insists, "is never achieved for its own sake. . . . Effectiveness of assertion is the Alpha and Omega of style. He who has nothing to assert has no style and can have none: he who has something to assert will go as far in power of style as its momentousness and his conviction will carry him."[69] More often than is usually recognized, Wilde had something momentous to assert.

The premise of Wilde's new ethical outlook, as of that of many of his contemporaries, is that human nature constantly changes; he rejects the traditional view of an immutable human nature. To those who say that "you can't change human nature," he replies that not only you can but you must.⁷⁰ Speaking with Lord Henry Wotton in *Dorian Gray,* Basil Hallward insists that one must pay for one's sins: "One has to pay in other ways than money," he says.

"What sort of ways, Basil?"

"Oh, I should fancy in remorse, in suffering, in . . . well, in the consciousness of degradation."

"My dear fellow," Lord Henry replies with a shrug of the shoulders, "medieval art is charming, but medieval emotions are out of date."⁷¹ Wilde's view was that expressed later by Norman Douglas that "you might as well say . . . that these cliffs never change" as to say that human nature never changes: "The proof that the laws of good conduct change is this, that if you were upright after the fashion of your great-grandfather you would soon find yourself in the clutches of the law for branding a slave, or putting a bullet through someone in a duel. . . . The Spartans, a highly moral people, thought it positively indecent not to steal. A modern vice, such as mendacity, was accounted a virtue by the greatest nation of antiquity. A modern virtue, like that of forgiving one's enemies, was accounted a vice proper to slaves. Drunkenness, reprobated by ancients and moderns alike, became the mark of a gentleman in intermediate periods."⁷² William Morris shares with Wilde this view of human nature as in a perpetual process of change; to a question about human nature in *News from Nowhere,* for example, Hammond replies with the query: *"Which* human nature?"⁷³

Wilde was not prepared to spell out the form human nature would be likely to take if men were able to live out their lives "fully and completely"; he had too intimate a sense that the personality is complex to the point of unknowability to make such an attempt. He speaks in *Dorian Gray* of the "shallow psychology of those who conceive the Ego in man as a thing simple, permanent, reliable, of one essence." "Only the shallow," he said, "know themselves."⁷⁴ A man whose aim is self-realization cannot possibly know in advance where he is going: "One whose desire is to be something separate from himself, to be a member of Parliament, or a successful grocer, or a prominent solicitor, or a judge, or something equally tedious, invariably succeeds in being what he wants to be. That is his punishment. . . . But with the dynamic forces of life, it is different. People whose desire is solely for self-realization never know where they are going. They can't know. . . . To recognize that the soul is unknowable is the ultimate achievement of wisdom."[75]

But for the present—partly, to be sure, because of his delight in shocking people of conventional principles, but also with an undertone of serious intention—he proposes a daring reversal of ethical norms. We are living in a time, he says, when "most people die of a sort of creeping common sense, and discover when it is too late that the only things one never regrets are one's mistakes."[76] At a time like this the experience society forbids is likely to be of the highest worth: "By its curiosity, sin increases the experience of the race. Through its intensified assertion of individualism, it saves us from monotony of type. In its rejection of the current notions about morality, it is one with the higher ethics."[77] "Modern morality," he says again, "consists in accepting the standard of one's age. I consider that for any man of culture to accept the standard of his age is a form of the grossest immorality."[78] In conformity with this principle, Wilde reverses the roles of duty and idleness, work and pleasure: "It is mentally and morally injurious to man to do anything in which he does not find pleasure," he says.[79] "Pleasure is Nature's test, her sign of approval. When we are happy we are always good, but when we are good we are not always happy."[80] To take one's business obligations seriously was to exhibit weakness of character: "I have known men come to London full of bright prospects and seen them complete wrecks in a few months through a habit of answering letters."[81] When Henley asked him how much time he put in at the office as editor of *Woman's World,* he replied, "I used to go three times a week, for an hour a day, but I have struck off one of the days."[82] In matters of the intellect as well as of morality, Wilde reverses the customary norms; it is the "dangerous" theory, he says, that is likely to have greatest worth.[83]

Wilde and Morris were at one in looking toward a time when the individual would go further toward self-realization than at present. But they were different in that Morris, unlike Wilde, was sure of what self-realization meant. In his ability to speak definitely about what the "perfected society" would be like, Morris, in fact, may be compared with Matthew Arnold. What man needs first of all, Morris says, is a correct attitude toward work. Work for him is never discipline, as it is for Carlyle; it is, and must be, pleasure; here he shows the influence of Ruskin's *Stones of Venice*. The kind of work most certain to give pleasure is creative work. Morris is no less certain than Arnold that in order to fulfill themselves men must find ways to discover and exercise their creativity. In *News from Nowhere* he tells us that for some years after the revolution "a kind of disappointment seemed coming over us, and the prophecies of some of the reactionists of past times seemed as if they would come true, and a dull level of utilitarian comfort be the end for a while of our aspirations and success."[84] But the people of *News from Nowhere* found their answer in creative activity, in art, whose function, as Morris sees it, is "to increase the happiness of men, by giving them beauty and interest of incident to amuse their leisure, and prevent them wearying even of rest, and by giving them hope and bodily pleasure in their work; or, shortly, to make man's work happy and his rest fruitful."[85] It is art for Morris that gives us, in his splendid phrase, "eager life while we live."[86] Another secret of the "full and complete" life, for Morris, is to learn to take an interest in the everyday events and occurrences of living: "It seems to me that a very real way to enjoy life is to accept all its necessary ordinary details and turn them into pleasures by taking an interest in them."[87] The people in *News from Nowhere,* for example, "were eager to discuss all the little details of life—the weather, the hay-crop, the last new house, the plenty or lack of such and such birds, and so on; and they talked of these things, not in a fatuous and conventional way, but as taking, I say, real interest in them."[88] In this they differed from people in the nineteenth century when even country people, Morris observes, could tell you little about the country. The final key to the good life for Morris is a right relationship with people: "Forsooth, brothers, fellowship is heaven, and lack of fellowship is hell: fellowship is life, and lack of fellowship is death: and the deeds that ye do upon the earth, it is for fellowship's sake that ye do them. . . ."[89] Morris's conception of a "full and complete" life is fit to stand by Arnold's as one of the luminous and satisfying formulations of human goals the nineteenth century produced. It was because Morris had won from experience wisdom of this character that Rossetti, who earlier had often mocked Morris as a kind of "hearty undergraduate," came to have "an uneasy consciousness that he was no longer that; that he had grown in dignity and even majesty of mind; that he was, in certain particulars, a stranger."[90] Wilde does not have a large body of tested wisdom of this sort to offer. He was too indolent, too much cut off from life, too much the poseur, to achieve this kind of maturity—though one must recall, too, that his life was blasted in mid-career, while Morris ripened in experience till the day of his death at sixty-two. Yet if Morris gives us a more usable conception of human goals than does Wilde, Wilde had a keener sense than Morris of the unrealized potentialities of experience.

In certain other respects, Wilde displayed a sanity and maturity worthy of Morris. He anticipated a number of ethical views which are only now, and slowly, gaining general acceptance, views that represent a major feature of the ethical advance that has run counter to so many decadent trends in the past half-century. One of these is the view that in certain situations the most productive attitude toward matters traditionally regarded as of right and wrong is one of ethical neutrality. Wilde understood something of what Freudian psychology has taught later generations as to how an excessively moral attitude toward experience may interfere with a right understanding of life. This knowledge he expressed in characteristic hyperbole when he said that "a color sense is more important, in the development of the individual, than a sense of right and wrong."[91] "I never approve or disapprove of anything now," says Henry Wotton in *Dorian Gray*. "It is an absurd attitude to take toward life. We are not sent into the world to air our moral prejudices."[92]

Still more important is Wilde's view that the goal of the moral life should be unification of the personality. "To be good," he says, "is to be in harmony with oneself."[93] When he speaks of harmony he has in mind, partly, healing of the rift between sense and spirit—the theme Rossetti treats in many of the *House of Life* sonnets: "Those who see any difference between soul and body," he says, "have neither."[94] But he has in mind, too, the healing of the rift between instinct and conscience: "The mere existence of conscience, that faculty of which people prate so much nowadays, and are so ignorantly proud, is a sign of our imperfect development; it must be merged in instinct before we become fine."[95] Here Wilde anticipates in quite extraordinary fashion an outlook that Freudian psychology has popularized; for what he is saying is that psychological maturity requires diminishing of the role of the *super-ego* and the *id* in favor of strong *ego* development. A remarkable passage in *De Profundis* shows that unification of the personality was not merely something Wilde talked about, but the deepest aim of his life. The laws under which he was convicted were unjust laws, he says, and the system an unjust system. "But, somehow," he goes on, "I have got to make both of these things just and right to me. And exactly as in Art one is only concerned with what a particular thing is at a particular moment to oneself, so it is also in the ethical evolution of one's character. I have got to make everything that has happened to me good for me. . . . The important thing, the thing that lies before me, the thing that I have to do, if the brief reminder of my days is not to be maimed, marred, and incomplete, is to absorb into my nature all that has been done to me, to make it part of me, to accept it without complaint, fear, or reluctance. The supreme vice is shallowness. Whatever is realized is right. . . . To regret one's own experiences is to arrest one's own development. To deny one's own experience is to put a lie into the lips of one's life. It is no less than a denial of the soul."[96]

Those who wish to find such a moral will have no difficulty in regarding Wilde's antinomian ethics as the source of the disaster of his life. He paid heavily for expressing ethical views in many ways ahead of, and always defiant of, those of his day. His punishment, W. Y. Tindall says, "was less the punishment of particular misdemeanors than the symbolic revenge of a class upon artists and their arts,"[97] but it was a revenge also upon a rebel against the established ethical system. While he did not work out his ideas with anything like completeness, he responded sufficiently to the expansive age in which he lived to sketch the outlines of a revolutionary ethic the history of which is even now far from completed. His place is secure as an initiator of a shift in orientation that marked the passing of one world and the birth of another.

Eight

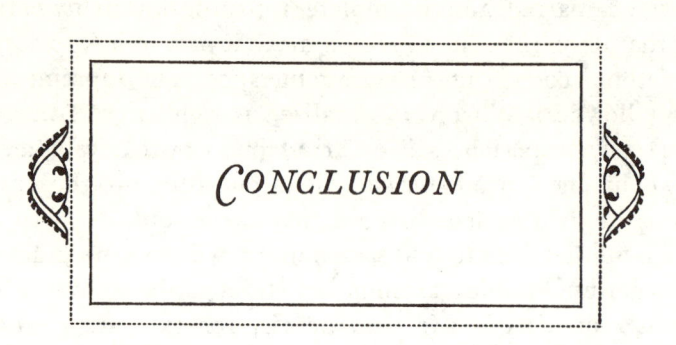

CONCLUSION

THE REFORM ACT OF 1832 PLACED IN COMMAND OF ENGLAND'S destinies the leaders of an industrial system more productive than anything before dreamed of. The new masters of England had the potential power, as they well knew, to give a reasonable degree of leisure and a sufficiency of the world's goods to the whole population. When they strove for power in the Reform Bill campaign, and later when they sought to confirm and extend their power in the anti-Corn Law agitation, members of this class proclaimed that they could furnish greater happiness to a greater number of people than any previous social order had been able to provide. They were not demagogues; the new industrialism did have this potentiality—provided, of course, that its productive power could be used in the interest of society as a whole.

A class that is expanding the system of production may come to regard itself, in a measure justifiably, as champion of the cause of humanity, custodian for the moment of the best features of the human inheritance. Matthew Arnold, skeptical as he was about the new governing class, gave the best account of the promise the new ruling class held for all humanity, when he wrote of the "perfected society" man now had it in his power to achieve. Though to describe the middle class he invented—or rather popularized—the term "Philistine," and though in his account of philistinism he employed all his powers of irony, he believed that for the foreseeable future the middle class would control England's destiny; the aristocracy he regarded as practically defunct, and the day of the working class, he felt, was as yet far off. He believed, too, that despite perils of which he was acutely aware, the destiny of England might yet be a glorious one. If in his satire on the classes and institutions of his day he mirrors the actuality, in his account of the perfected society he mirrors the creative potentialities of the new order. Uniting in this account as he does the best features of Greek civilization, the Renaissance, Puritanism and the eighteenth century, prophesying a time when the powers of knowledge, beauty, conduct, and manners will have the widest scope for development, Arnold speaks with greater eloquence than any other author of his time on the theme of what the new age had it in its power to achieve. Arnold's empiricism, his flexibility, his freedom from fixed conceptions, his readiness to submit all institutions and prescriptive rights to the test of experience embodied the best features of a class that was for the moment performing a creative role, dissolving the fixed institutions of the past in order to make possible a richer future.

But there were other aspects of the new society besides its glorious promise. The manufacturing class which had given assurance during the reform agitation that it could relieve the plight of the poor, failed for the time being at least to do so. Carlyle and Ruskin, like Engels and Marx, were agreed that the new wage-slavery surpassed in horror any other form of slavery known in modern times. When it became clear that the new order was not diminishing the hardships of the poor, but in some ways augmenting them, there began a movement of protest which expressed itself in the anti-Poor Law agitation and in Chartism, and then, after a period of stability following the mid-point of the century, in the socialist agitation of the eighties and nineties. While at times the movement of protest was little more than a blind revolt against unbearable conditions, at other times it was conscious of its aims. These aims, as formulated by the leaders of the London Working Men's Association in the eighteen-thirties, by the Chartists in the thirties and forties, and by the socialists in the eighties and nineties, were to continue institutional change beyond the point where the manufacturing class chose to halt it, and in so doing to proceed in the direction of economic democracy. A further peril in the new system lay in the fact that not the precepts of the political economists, as Carlyle and Ruskin believed, but the practices which the new industrial order brought into being, were producing a new kind of human nature. The new order magnified acquisitive motivation at the expense of altruism and fraternity, or brought about a split between the two kinds of motivation, the acquisitive being confined to one set of relationships (and week days) and the altruistic and fraternal to another set of relationships (and Sunday).

The perils of the new society were accurately diagnosed and powerfully assailed by Carlyle at the outset of the new period, and by Ruskin during the decades of its peak prosperity. Both writers brought to their criticism of industrialism an intensity of feeling attributable in part to the anxiety with which a neurotic nature responds to a threat to its precariously sustained ideals, for in both instances the social relationships of industrialism were in the sharpest contrast with an image of human relations which performed an indispensable role in the author's personality. Much of the power and acumen of the social criticism of both authors, then, is to be explained in terms of their personal psychology. To this source is to be ascribed also the failure of both Carlyle and Ruskin to formulate a satisfactory social philosophy such as might have enabled them successfully to complement the denunciation of abuses in whch they displayed such power.

In both authors fear of instinctual forces expressed itself in distrust of the drive of the masses toward fulfillment; in both, the need for a secure principle of authority within the personality expressed itself in the conviction that society, to maintain stability, required a principle of authority equally rigorous. Carlyle's distrust of instinct and his need for authority led him eventually to a contempt for ordinary humanity that alienates most readers today, to condemnation of democratic principle and the parliamentary process, to adulation of the hero, and advocacy of the gospel of salvation through renunciation, obedience, and work. Early in his career, before *Sartor Resartus,* Carlyle adopted a complex of authoritarian attitudes as a means of dealing with neurotic conflict. These attitudes he maintained throughout his life, the revolt of instinct making itself felt in hostility, depression, and loneliness, not in any weakening of the mechanism of control. In Ruskin, however, formidable personality conflicts manifested themselves later than with Carlyle, and Ruskin did not, like Carlyle, develop a consistent way of dealing with them. In his social attitudes, in consequence, he exhibits now trust in, now fear of the people, depending upon whether spontaneous drives or repressive forces are for the moment uppermost. But the only solution to the personal problem which offered Ruskin anything approaching security was to strengthen the principle of repression and control, and in his social philosophy authoritarianism became in consequence almost as prominent as in Carlyle's, though less consistently exhibited.

The likeness between Carlyle and Ruskin tempts one to suggest a generalization as to a necessary relationship between an authoritarian personality structure and a conservative political philosophy. But the fact is that the same personal characteristics are to be observed in those political revolutionaries who are driven by psychic revolt to struggle against authority in the state but are also driven by their need for inner authority to set up a new principle of rigorous political control. Many of the revolutionaries of the seventeenth century were probably men with this kind of psychological make-up, and the type is not unknown today. Similarly, one cannot generalize that persons with strong *ego* development—those who are able comfortably to handle their own spontaneity and who can make and carry out plans without neurotic interference—must necessarily adopt a democratic philosophy. These tempting simplifications must be avoided. A background of privilege, for example, by making possible a sense of mastery of the environment, contributes to strong *ego* development, but at the same time privilege is likely to predispose the individual to a conservative political philosophy. A background of privation, similarly, by depriving the individual of the power to handle his environment with competence and freedom, may impair *ego* development, but at the same time privation will often predispose the individual to a radical political philosophy. Perhaps the only safe generalization that can be made, therefore, is that other things being equal a man who has strength enough to trust himself will trust his fellow men and will therefore find a democratic outlook congenial, while a person with highly developed *super-ego,* who fears his instinctive nature, is likely to distrust ordinary humanity and to feel the need for a strong authority within society, and he may well, therefore, like Carlyle and Ruskin, adopt an antidemocratic political philosophy.

When contrasted with Carlyle and Ruskin, Matthew Arnold impresses one as a person of normal and healthy impulses. The distinction between normality and abnormality cannot be made to rest on the absence or presence of neurotic trends, for these exist in some form or other in most people. A normal person should be regarded rather as one who is able to think and act independently, without significant interference by inner drives over which he lacks control. An abnormal person is one whose thought and actions are to a significant degree determined, not by the

CONCLUSION 173

ego, which is imperfectly developed, but by the *super-ego* and *id*, and the mode through which he strives to resolve the conflict between them and gain security. Even with this distinction we cannot always classify people as normal or abnormal, but must rather say usually that a man is normal in some respects and abnormal in others—this being the condition, no doubt, of most of us. Yet if we adopt this distinction, we can say that Arnold (despite the cleavage in his nature), the young Rossetti (before the guilt obsession took hold of him), and Wilde (despite the impulse toward self-destruction and the morbid interest in "sin") were normal, and that Carlyle, Ruskin, and Thomson were not.

But psychic normality is not enough. One needs also the kind of relationship with society that will release and organize one's potentialties as an individual. Arnold failed to achieve such a relationship because he could not free himself from an ambivalent attitude toward the forces of expansion in modern times. He looked upon them, on the one hand, with warmth and confidence, for he believed that they had it in their power to prepare the way for the "perfected society"; but on the other hand he regarded them with anxiety, for he feared that, unless carefully guided and curbed, they would lead to the vulgarization of society, or, worse still, to anarchy and the mob spirit. The ambivalence widened the psychological cleavage in Arnold in two ways. It did so directly, in that Arnold's affirmative response to the "modern spirit" strengthened the expansive forces of his nature, while the negative response intensified the repressive forces. It did so indirectly, in that the philosophy through which Arnold sought to reconcile the conflicting responses to the age was necessarily so guarded and cautious that it failed to serve as a medium, as a satisfactory philosophy must, through which his emotional nature could freely express itself.

The more important result of Arnold's ambivalence is that while he is supreme in his account of the goals of human development, when it comes to making practical proposals as to how to advance toward the perfected society, his thinking requires much qualification and revision if it is to be of use to us. Arnold developed a philosophy designed to answer the needs of both sides of his nature, to assure him on the one hand that the forward movement toward the perfected society would proceed, and to assure him on the other hand that it would not proceed too fast. He urged a transformation of the spirit of society, therefore, through culture—the study of perfection, the development of our best selves, the utilization of the best that has been thought and known in the world. The agency of change was to be intellectual and spiritual influence alone; changes in social structure, perilous operations as Arnold saw them, were to be held up till the spiritual transformation was complete. But today we are not ready to concede that changes in society and in the spirit of society are brought about in the way Arnold supposed. In the thinking about social questions that supports his advocacy of culture, Arnold assumes that ideas in themselves can bring about results which in the opinion of most people today can be achieved only through alteration of the structure of society. Much of Arnold's critical analysis is in this way invalidated for our time. Acting as he does on the premise that the actions of men are governed by ideas rather than by the social relationships in which they find themselves, Arnold sometimes makes one think of a man trying to stop a riot by playing gentle music to the combatants instead of by trying to diagnose and eradicate the causes of the quarrel.

In a sense the reason for the failure in constructive criticism was the same for Carlyle, Ruskin, and Arnold. These authors had only a limited trust in people and were consequently unwilling to commit themselves to the democratic solution of the problem before them. It may well be that the only workable solution to the problem all these critics faced was an extension of democracy, through economic

CONCLUSION

as well as political measures, to the large masses excluded from its benefits. Ruskin and Carlyle were unable to advocate this approach to the problem of the age because of a psychic nature that developed in each of them a profound distrust of people. Arnold was unable to advocate it, not because of neurotic distrust of people, but because his point of view was sufficiently close to that of the middle class so that he shared its fear of democracy as well as its faith in it. In all three authors we encounter a failure to develop a structure of ideas fitted to serve as an instrument for the idealism they possessed. This is the first symptom, perhaps, of that inability of modern man to cope with his environment which has now become apparent to almost everyone. It is perhaps significant that Arnold was one of the first to speak of Europe's "dying hour."

All three authors, partly because of the failure to develop a satisfactory constructive philosophy, devoted themselves to the effort to transform the individual, Carlyle and Ruskin characteristically through invectives against Mammonism and avarice, Arnold through an appeal to the best self and advocacy of the study of perfection. Read today, these appeals to the individual appear as misconceived as Ruskin's sermons appeared to the *Spectator* reviewer mentioned earlier. We do not have here a personal appeal intended to enlist the individual in a struggle to change the structure of society, as in the seventeenth century; we do not have a personal appeal intended merely to change the individual within the context of a society not regarded as in need of change, as in the eighteenth century; we have an appeal, rather, that is intended to achieve results that only a change in social structure could accomplish, but with the intent to leave the social structure untouched. This it is that gives a considerable portion of the thought of the nineteenth century a quality that sometimes strikes one as perverse impotence.

Important as was the problem of adjustment to the breakdown of religious belief in the nineteenth century, its role was generally secondary, not primary. The main problem was one of social relationships, not of beliefs. It was because the problem of belief concealed a problem of social relationships that it often appeared of primary significance. Traditionally, religious belief had prescribed and clarified all personal and social relationships, answered all questions, defined all possible goals. It was to be expected, therefore, that when compelled to abandon belief, men should endeavor to construct a social philosophy to furnish a new framework for personal adjustment. None of the authors surveyed here, one notes, were men of orthodox faith. Carlyle, with his transcendentalism, and Arnold, with his "stream of tendency" God, sought to preserve certain religious values without dogma. Ruskin abandoned Evangelical belief in middle life. Thomson was an atheist, Rossetti a pagan with a nostalgia for the "mutter of the mass," Wilde a pagan without nostalgia. Those who in the nineteenth century were tortured by the loss of faith were generally, as was pointed out in the chapter on James Thomson, men who could find no way to deal with the self-assertive forces in the personality or with the struggle for fulfillment in society, without the inner and outer restraints religion provided, belief in the moral law and the duty of the poor to bear patiently the burden God had placed upon them. Those who did not feel this need to cling to belief because of its psychological or social function were generally able to achieve a satisfactory adjustment to society outside the framework of religion.

James Thomson was not, however. The main reason was that he identified himself with a radical movement at a time when conditions were less favorable to a radical program than at any other period in the century—a movement, too, quite powerless to rally and organize the minority who were then ready to respond to a radical appeal. Thomson was hardheaded enough to comprehend the inadequacy of the Secularist program, though this understanding took the form of a theoretical disbelief in the efficacy of any kind of reform movement. Thomson failed to develop a satisfactory relationship to his age, then, mainly because he lived at a time when the only available social philosophy that came near to answering his needs was one to which only a more naïve man than he could give wholehearted support. Thomson's failure in adjustment to society, however, is to be regarded as a contributory cause of a pessimism that in the main must be accounted for in terms of psychic abnormality.

If Carlyle's thought is to be associated mainly with the thirties and forties, and Arnold's and Ruskin's with the fifties, sixties, and seventies, then Thomson's is to be associated with the seventies, Rossetti's with the seventies, eighties, and nineties, and Wilde's with the eighties and nineties. One can name the seventies, eighties, and nineties for Rossetti because, though his characteristic attitudes took shape as early as 1848, and though he died in 1882, the estheticism for which he stands as a central symbol belongs primarily to these last three decades of the century. In Rossetti we encounter for the first time in England a phenomenon that has since become common, that of the artist who deliberately turns away from a society he regards as regimented, ugly, and hypocritical in order to create for himself a private religion of beauty. It was because he lacked the principle of integration and the clarification of purpose that are to be achieved only through vital social relationships that Rossetti clung so long to the dream of ideal love, and it is for this reason too that he became a prey to feelings of guilt and remorse that a maturer personality would have been able to subordinate or curb.

In Rossetti, as in Arnold, an unsatisfactory relationship to society contributed to the development of psychological difficulties—in Arnold to the sense of cleavage already discussed, in Rossetti to manifestations of guilt of a sort generally attributable to neurosis. In these two authors, therefore, we encounter a phenomenon opposite to that of which Carlyle, Ruskin, and Thomson are examples. In Carlyle, Ruskin, and Thomson, psychological difficulties were sufficiently acute to stand in the way of social adjustment, but in Arnold and Rossetti a failure in social adjustment is the cause of psychological difficulties. In all five authors, to be sure, the interaction between psychological and social causation is so close that to look upon one set of trends exclusively as cause and the other exclusively as effect must represent an oversimplification. But we are justified in saying that in Carlyle, Ruskin, and Thomson (in so far as Thomson's difficulty was of neurotic origin) psychological abnormality of the kind that has its roots in childhood led to difficulties in social adjustment, while in Arnold and Rossetti difficulties in social adjustment—of the kind that are to be explained entirely in terms of adult experience—led to psychological difficulties. In a different society Carlyle, Ruskin and Thomson would still have faced severe difficulties in adjustment, but Arnold and Rossetti would not.

Thomson is important in literature mainly because of the monumental and impressive weight of his projection of a pessimistic philosophy, Rossetti because of his rare artifice, the intensity and power with which he handles such themes as the dream of ideal love and the oneness of sense and soul, and the controlled luxuriance of his imagery and diction. Impairment of a man's psychic or social functioning does not prevent his achieving great distinction in literature. But it does prevent him from doing work of the first order. Thomson and Rossetti are not among the very great authors; their work, valuable as it is, lacks qualities of relevance and power that only more complete and mature experience than theirs can give.

In the eighties and nineties the established order was shaken by a major depression, and a movement of protest arose which combined a new confidence in the potentialties of human society with the conviction that a change in the structure of society had become imperative. The new outlook made it possible for many, of whom Morris and Shaw are the most eminent literary examples, to relate themselves to society in a way that had not previously been possible, except for a few. Wilde's share in the new vision of the last decades, along with the strength of the principle of spontaneity in the man, was the source of a revolutionary ethical outlook which makes of him—esthete, poseur, and decadent as he was in the main—one of the significant initiators of a new age.

The most pressing problems in America at the moment are different from those that give a kind of unity to the work of these nineteenth-century British authors. Yet beneath the difference, a similarity remains. These authors constitute a capital part of our literary inheritance both because of the direct influence they exert and because of the similarities between the problems they faced and ours. In some ways the changes of the intervening years have made it even harder for us than it was for them to overcome the almost unsurmountable obstacles that for modern man stand in the way of a productive life. But in other ways the task should be easier for us—if only because we have their diverse and rich experience on which to draw.

NOTES

One

INTRODUCTION

1. James L. Halliday, *Mr. Carlyle: My Patient—A Psychosomatic Biography* (New York: Grune and Stratton, 1950).
2. Amabel Williams-Ellis, *An Exquisite Tragedy: An Intimate Life of John Ruskin* (Garden City, N. Y.: Doubleday Doran, 1929).
3. R. H. Wilenski, *John Ruskin: an Introduction to Further Study of His Life and Work* (New York: Frederick A. Stokes, 1933).
4. Erich Fromm, *Escape from Freedom* (New York: Farrar and Rinehart, 1941), pp. 250-51.

Two

THOMAS CARLYLE

1. James Anthony Froude, *Thomas Carlyle: a History of His Life in London* (London: Longmans, Green, 1890), I, 41.
2. E. Vaughan, "Carlyle and his German Masters," *Essays and*

Studies by Members of the English Association (Oxford: Clarendon Press, 1910), pp. 184-88.
3. J. L. and Barbara Hammond, *Lord Shaftesbury* (London: Constable and Company, 1925), p. 10.
4. Barnard N. Schilling, *Human Dignity and the Great Victorians* (New York: Columbia University Press, 1946), p. 9.
5. *Ibid.*, p. 10.
6. Miriam M. H. Thrall, *Rebellious Fraser's* (New York: Columbia University Press, 1934), p. 138.
7. Bertrand Russell, *Freedom versus Organization, 1814-1914* (New York: W. W. Norton, 1934), p. 74.
8. G. D. H. Cole and Raymond Postgate, *The British Common People: 1746-1938* (New York: Knopf, 1939), p. 278.
9. *Ibid.*, p. 245.
10. G. M. Young, *Early Victorian England, 1830-1865* (London: Oxford University Press, 1934), II, 443.
11. John Stuart Mill, *The Spirit of the Age,* ed. Frederick A. von Hayek (Chicago: University of Chicago Press, 1942), pp. 91-92.
12. Russell, *op. cit.*, p. 121.
13. Hesketh Pearson, *The Smith of Smiths, being the Life, Wit, and Humor of Sydney Smith* (New York: Harper & Brothers, 1934), p. 45.
14. Cole and Postgate, *op. cit.*, pp. 300 ff.
15. *Ibid.*, pp. 233-35.
16. J. L. and Barbara Hammond, *op. cit.*, p. 101.
17. Charles Dickens, *Complete Works* (London: Chapman and Hall, 1874), IX, 371 (*Hard Times*).
18. Friedrich Engels, *The Condition of the Working Class in England in 1844* (New York: J. W. Lovell Co., 1887), p. 190.
19. J. L. and Barbara Hammond, *op. cit.*, p. 24.
20. Thrall, *op. cit.*, p. 129.
21. J. L. and Barbara Hammond, *op. cit.*, p. 30.
22. *Ibid.*, p. 33.
23. Dickens, *Works,* IX, 367-68 (*Hard Times*).
24. *Ibid.*, IX, 373.
25. Cole and Postgate, *op. cit.*, p. 230.
26. S. Maccoby, *English Radicalism: 1832-1852* (London: Allen and Unwin, 1935), p. 45.
27. James Anthony Froude, *Thomas Carlyle: a History of the First Forty Years of His Life, 1795-1835* (London: Longmans, Green, 1891), II, 210.

28. Elie Halévy, *A History of the British People: 1830-1841* (New York: Harcourt, Brace, 1924), p. 293.
29. Cole and Postgate, *op. cit.*, p. 237.
30. William Morris, *Signs of Change: Seven Lectures* (London: Longmans, Green, 1913), p. 111.
31. Cole and Postgate, *op. cit.*, pp. 176-77.
32. Froude, *Thomas Carlyle: First Forty Years*, II, 84.
33. Thrall, *op. cit.*, p. 129.
34. Froude, *Thomas Carlyle: Life in London*, I, 183.
35. Froude, *Thomas Carlyle: First Forty Years*, I, 389.
36. *Ibid.*, II, 79-80.
37. *Ibid.*, II, 157.
38. *Ibid.*, II, 239.
39. Froude, *Thomas Carlyle: Life in London*, I, 362.
40. Froude, *Thomas Carlyle: First Forty Years*, II, 312.
41. Froude, *Thomas Carlyle: Life in London*, I, 312.
42. J. Bruce Glasier, *William Morris and the Early Years of the Socialist Movement* (London: Longmans, Green, 1921), p. 67.
43. Mark Hovell, *The Chartist Movement* (Manchester, England: Manchester University Press, 1925), p. 46.
44. *Ibid.*, pp. 53-54.
45. *Ibid.*, p. 57.
46. *Ibid.*, p. 85.
47. *Ibid.*, p. 1.
48. Herbert Spencer, *An Autobiography* (New York: D. Appleton, 1904), I, 440.
49. *Ibid.*, I, 443.
50. Harriet Martineau, *Autobiography* (London: Smith, Elder and Company, 1877), I, 381.
51. Froude, *Thomas Carlyle: Life in London*, I, 238.
52. *Ibid.*, I, 299.
53. *Ibid.*, II, 132.
54. Froude, *Thomas Carlyle: First Forty Years*, II, 50.
55. Froude, *Thomas Carlyle: Life in London*, I, 20.
56. *Ibid.*, II, 85.
57. *Ibid.*, II, 16.
58. Froude, *Thomas Carlyle: First Forty Years*, II, 266.
59. Jackson E. Towne, "Carlyle and Oedipus," *The Psychoanalytic Review*, XXII (1935), 297.
60. Herbert Paul, *Life of James Anthony Froude* (New York: Scribner's, 1905), p. 300.

61. Halliday, *Mr. Carlyle, My Patient*, p. 81.
62. Fromm, *Escape from Freedom*, p. 173.
63. *Ibid.*, pp. 90-91.
64. Froude, *Thomas Carlyle: Life in London*, I, p. 73.
65. *Ibid.*, I, 115.
66. Emery Neff, *Carlyle and Mill: an Introduction to Victorian Thought* (New York: Columbia University Press, 1926), pp. 26-27.
67. Froude, *Thomas Carlyle: Life in London*, II, 4.
68. *Ibid.*, II, 353.
69. *Ibid.*, I, 454.
70. *Ibid.*, I, 401.
71. Oliver Elton, *A Survey of English Literature, 1780-1880* (New York: Macmillan, 1920), III, 17.
72. Froude, *Thomas Carlyle: Life in London*, I, 187.
73. George Bernard Shaw, *Collected Works* (New York: Wm. H. Wise, 1930-32), X, 218 ("Maxims for Revolutionaries" appended to *Man and Superman*).
74. Froude, *Thomas Carlyle: Life in London*, I, 117.
75. *Ibid.*, II, 22.
76. Shaw, *Works*, X, 206 ("The Revolutionist's Handbook and Pocket Companion" appended to *Man and Superman*).
77. Froude, *Thomas Carlyle: Life in London*, I, 38.
78. *Ibid.*, II, 28.
79. *Ibid.*, I, 390.
80. *Ibid.*, I, 433.
81. *Ibid.*, I, 297.
82. Froude, *Thomas Carlyle: First Forty Years*, II, 211.
83. Froude, *Thomas Carlyle: Life in London*, I, 15.
84. Mill, *op. cit.*, p. xxii.
85. Pearson, *op. cit.*, p. 23.
86. Thrall, *op. cit.*, p. 129.
87. Halévy, *op. cit.*, p. 294.
88. J. L. and Barbara Hammond, *op. cit.*, p. 14.
89. Froude, *Thomas Carlyle: First Forty Years*, I, 191.
90. Pearson, *op. cit.*, p. 106.
91. Froude, *Thomas Carlyle: Life in London*, I, 369.
92. Quoted by Basil Willey, *Nineteenth Century Studies* (London: Chatto and Windus, 1949), p. 128.
93. Quoted by Willey, *op. cit.*, pp. 128-29.

Three

MATTHEW ARNOLD

1. *Letters of Matthew Arnold,* ed. George W. E. Russell (London: Macmillan, 1904), II, 260. Letter to his mother, 1871.
2. *Letters,* I, 14.
3. Kenneth Burke, *The Philosophy of Literary Form: Studies in Symbolic Action* (Baton Rouge: Louisiana State University Press, 1941), p. 64.
4. *Letters of Matthew Arnold to Arthur Hugh Clough,* ed. Howard Foster Lowry (New York: Oxford University Press, 1932), p. 124.
5. C. B. Tinker and H. F. Lowry, *The Poetry of Matthew Arnold: a Commentary* (London: Oxford University Press, 1940), p. 270.
6. *Letters,* I, 14.
7. *Letters to Clough,* p. 110. Letter of September 23, 1849.
8. *Ibid.,* p. 63. Letter of 1847.
9. Matthew Arnold, "On the Modern Element in Literature," *Macmillan's Magazine,* XIX (Feb., 1869), 305.
10. *Matthew Arnold's Notebooks,* with a preface by the Hon. Mrs. Wodehouse (New York: Macmillan, 1902), p. 28.
11. *The Works of Matthew Arnold* (London: Macmillan, 1903-4), X, 44 (*Mixed Essays*).
12. *Works,* VI, 29 (*Culture and Anarchy*).
13. *Works,* VI, 30 (*Culture and Anarchy*).
14. Matthew Arnold, *England and the Italian Question* (London: Longmans, Green, 1859), p. 10.
15. Matthew Arnold, *Civilization in the United States: First and Last Impressions of America* (Boston: Cupples and Hurd, 1888), p. 145.
16. *England and the Italian Question,* p. 30.
17. *Works,* X, 14 (*Mixed Essays*).
18. *Works,* X, 44 (*Mixed Essays*).
19. *Works,* XI, 142 (*Irish Essays*).
20. *Works,* III, 235 (*Essays in Criticism*).
21. *Works,* VI, 139 (*Culture and Anarchy*).
22. *Works,* VI, 393-94 ("My Countrymen").
23. *Notebooks,* p. 57.
24. *Works,* X, 63-64 (*Mixed Essays*).

25. *Works*, III, 242 (*Essays in Criticism*).
26. *Works*, X, 45 (*Mixed Essays*).
27. *Works*, III, 332 (*Essays in Criticism*).
28. *Works*, III, 18 (*Essays in Criticism*).
29. *England and the Italian Question*, pp. 29-30.
30. *Letters*, III, 59-60.
31. *Letters*, I, 324-25.
32. *Works*, VI, 367 ("My Countrymen").
33. *England and the Italian Question*, p. 29.
34. *Civilization in the United States*, p. 116.
35. *Ibid.*, p. 127.
36. *Letters*, II, 62.
37. *Civilization in the United States*, p. 136.
38. *Ibid.*, pp. 145-46.
39. *Works*, XII, 83 (*A French Eton*).
40. Frederic Harrison, *Tennyson, Ruskin, Mill and Other Literary Estimates* (New York: Macmillan, 1900), p. 124.
41. *Works*, X, vi (*Mixed Essays*).
42. *Works*, VI, 20-21 (*Culture and Anarchy*).
43. *Works*, III, 4 (*Essays in Criticism*).
44. *Works*, XII, 83 (*A French Eton*).
45. *Works*, III, 44 (*Essays in Criticism*).
46. Schilling, *Human Dignity and the Great Victorians*, p. 10.
47. Elizabeth Gaskell, *Mary Barton* (New York: E. P. Dutton, 1924), p. 81.
48. Halévy, *History of the British People: 1830-1841*, p. 303.
49. *Ibid.*, p. 305.
50. *Ibid.*, p. 319.
51. Cole and Postgate, *The British Common People: 1746-1938*, p. 300.
52. Russell, *Freedom versus Organization*, p. 175.
53. Maccoby, *English Radicalism: 1853-1886*, p. 98.
54. J. L. and Barbara Hammond, *Lord Shaftesbury*, p. 86.
55. Gaskell, *op. cit.*, p. x.
56. *Ibid.*, p. 79.
57. *Ibid.*, p. 2.
58. Frances Wentworth Knickerbocker, *Free Minds: John Morley and his Friends* (Cambridge: Harvard University Press, 1943), p. 8.
59. Michael Sadleir, *Trollope: a Commentary* (New York: Farrar, Straus, 1947), p. 20.
60. Cole and Postgate, *op. cit.*, p. 245.

61. Paul, *Life of Froude,* p. 47.
62. Arthur V. Woodworth, *Christian Socialism in England* (London: Swan Sonnenschein and Co., 1903), p. 9.
63. *Ibid.,* p. 12.
64. J. L. and Barbara Hammond, *op. cit.,* pp. 67-68.
65. Cole and Postgate, *op. cit.,* pp. 330-31.
66. Halévy, *op. cit.,* p. 308.
67. John Morley, *The Life of Richard Cobden* (London: Macmillan, 1908), I, 153.
68. *Ibid.,* I, 153.
69. Russell, *op. cit.,* p. 127.
70. Morley, *op. cit.,* I, 154.
71. *Ibid.,* I, 155.
72. *Ibid.,* I, 248.
73. *Ibid.,* I, 169.
74. Halévy, *op. cit.,* p. 313.
75. *Ibid.,* p. 316.
76. Morley, *op. cit.,* I, 166-168.
77. *Ibid.,* I, 226, 228.
78. Maccoby, *op. cit.,* p. 405.
79. *Ibid.,* p. 405.
80. *Ibid.,* p. 228.
81. Maccoby, *English Radicalism: 1832-1852,* p. 8.
82. *Letters,* I, 5. Letter to his mother, March 7, 1848.
83. *Letters to Clough,* p. 77.
84. *Letters,* I, 7.
85. *Letters,* I, 66.
86. *Works,* X, 44 ("Democracy," *Mixed Essays*).
87. *Works,* III, 12 (*Essays in Criticism*).
88. *Works,* III, 13 (*Essays in Criticism*).
89. *Works,* III, 328-29 (*Essays in Criticism*).
90. *Works,* VI, xxxix (*Culture and Anarchy,* Preface of 1869).
91. *Works,* VI, 11 (*Culture and Anarchy*).
92. *Works,* VI, 41 (*Culture and Anarchy*).
93. *Works,* VI, 158 (*Culture and Anarchy*).
94. *Works,* VI, 36 (*Culture and Anarchy*).
95. *Works,* VI, 71 (*Culture and Anarchy*).
96. William Morris, *News from Nowhere, or an Epoch of Rest* (London: Longmans, Green, 1917), p. 157.
97. *Works,* VI, 216 (*Culture and Anarchy*).
98. *Works,* X, 83-84 ("Equality," *Mixed Essays*).
99. *Works,* X, 65 ("Equality,"*Mixed Essays*).

100. *Works*, X, 91 ("Equality," *Mixed Essays*).
101. "A Word More about America," *Civilization in the United States*, pp. 135-36.
102. *Works*, IV, 309 ("Numbers," *Discourses in America*).
103. "The Nadir of Liberalism," *The Nineteenth Century*, XIX, no. 111 (May, 1886), 647.
104. *Ibid.*, p. 654.
105. *Ibid.*, p. 650.
106. *Works*, XI, 24 (*Irish Essays*); see also "The Zenith of Conservatism," *The Nineteenth Century*, XXI, no. 119 (Jan., 1887), p. 161.
107. "The Nadir of Liberalism," p. 655.
108. *Letters*, III, 45.
109. John Morley, "Plain Story of the Zulu War," *Fortnightly Review*, XXXI (March, 1879), 348.
110. John Morley, "Further Remarks on Zulu Affairs," *Fortnightly Review*, XXXI (April, 1879), 547.
111. *Ibid.*, p. 562.
112. Morris, *News from Nowhere*, pp. 131-32.
113. Morris, *Signs of Change*, p. 92.
114. Glasier, *William Morris and the Early Days of the Socialist Movement*, p. 101.
115. George Saintsbury, *Matthew Arnold* (New York: Dodd, Mead, 1899).
116. Leonard Woolf, *After the Deluge: a Study of Communal Psychology* (New York: Harcourt Brace, 1931), pp. 281-87.
117. Ernest Barker, *Political Thought in England from Herbert Spencer to the Present Day* (New York: Henry Holt, 1916), pp. 198-99.
118. J. Dover Wilson, "Matthew Arnold and the Educationists," in *The Social and Political Ideas of Some Representative Thinkers of the Victorian Age*, ed. F. J. C. Hearnshaw (London: G. C. Harrap, 1933), p. 168.
119. Lionel Trilling, *Matthew Arnold* (New York: W. W. Norton, 1939), p. 279.
120. Howard Mumford Jones, "Arnold, Aristocracy, and America," *American Historical Review*, XLIX (April, 1944), pp. 393-409.
121 Knickerbocker, *op. cit.*, p. 56.
122. "The Buried Life."
123. *Idem*.
124. "Obermann."

125. "The Scholar Gypsy."
126. Fromm, *Escape from Freedom*, p. 36.
127. Aldous Huxley, "Wordsworth in the Tropics," *Rotunda* (London: Chatto and Windus, 1932), p. 881.
128. Trilling, *op. cit.*, p. 178.
129. *Works*, VI, 316 (*Friendship's Garland*).
130. *Works*, VI, 41 (*Culture and Anarchy*).
131. *Works*, III, 12 (*Essays in Criticism*).
132. *Works*, III, 30 (*Essays in Criticism*).
133. *Works*, V, 150 (*On the Study of Celtic Literature*).
134. *Works*, VI, xii (*Culture and Anarchy*).
135. *Works*, VI, 8 (*Culture and Anarchy*).
136. *Works*, VI, 46 (*Culture and Anarchy*).
137. *Works*, XI, 38 (*Irish Essays*).
138. "The Nadir of Liberalism," p. 645.
139. *Works*, III, 20-21 (*Essays in Criticism*).
140. George Saintsbury, *Matthew Arnold* (New York: Dodd, Mead, 1899).
141. Edward Killoran Brown, *Matthew Arnold: A Study in Conflict* (Chicago: University of Chicago Press, 1948).
142. *Works*, VI, 371 ("My Countrymen").
143. *Works*, X, 6 (*Mixed Essays*).
144. *Works*, III, 44 ("The Function of Criticism at the Present Time," *Essays in Criticism*).
145. *Works*, VI, 158 (*Culture and Anarchy*).
146. *Letters to Clough*, p. 142.
147. *Works*, III, 14 (*Essays in Criticism*).
148. *Works*, III, 11 (*Essays in Criticism*).
149. *Works*, III, 14 (*Essays in Criticism*).
150. *Works*, III, 13 (*Essays in Criticism*).
151. *Works*, X, 75-76 (*Mixed Essays*).
152. *Works*, V, 317-18 (*Friendship's Garland*).
153. *Works*, X, 30 (*Mixed Essays*).

Four

JOHN RUSKIN

1. *The Complete Works of John Ruskin* (Philadelphia: Reuwee, Wattlee and Walsh, 1891), V, 357 (*The Study of Architecture*).

2. E. T. Cook, *The Life of John Ruskin* (London: Allen, 1911), II, 19-20.
3. William Gaunt, *The Pre-Raphaelite Tragedy* (New York: Harcourt, Brace, 1942), p. 175.
4. Williams-Ellis, *The Exquisite Tragedy: an Intimate Life of John Ruskin*, p. 76.
5. *Ibid.*, p. 86.
6. *Letters of John Ruskin to Charles Eliot Norton*, ed. Charles Eliot Norton (Boston: Houghton, Mifflin, 1904), I, 17.
7. Thomas Earle Welby, *A Study of Swinburne* (London: Faber and Gwyer, 1926), p. 19.
8. Wilenski, *John Ruskin: an Introduction to Further Study of His Life and Work*.
9. Louis J. Bragman, "The Case of John Ruskin: A Study of Cyclothymia," *American Journal of Psychiatry*, 91 (March, 1935), 1137-59.
10. T. M. Mitchell, review of R. H. Wilenski's *John Ruskin* in *British Journal of Medical Psychology*, XIII (December, 1933), 354-59.
11. Louise A. Nelson, "Why John Ruskin Never Learned How to Live," *Mental Hygiene*, XII (October, 1928), 673-705.
12. *Works*, XIV, 203 (*Time and Tide*).
13. *Works*, IX, Letter LVIII (*Fors Clavigera*).
14. *Works*, XIV, 170 (*Time and Tide*).
15. *Works*, XIV, 217 (*Time and Tide*).
16. *Works*, XIV, 189 (*Time and Tide*).
17. *Works*, XVIII, 270 (*Arrows of the Chase*).
18. Quoted by Evelyn Waugh, *Rossetti, His Life and Work* (London: Duckworth, 1928), p. 69.
19. *Works*, XIV, 133 (*Time and Tide*).
20. Bragman, *op. cit.*, p. 1158.
21. *Works*, XIV, 197 (*Time and Tide*).
22. *Works*, VIII, Letter XLVIII (*Fors Clavigera*).
23. *Works*, VI, 208 (*Unto This Last*).
24. *Works*, XII, 272 (*Lectures on Art*).
25. *Works*, XV, 63 (*The Crown of Wild Olive*).
26. *Works*, VI, 175-76 (*Unto This Last*).
27. *Works*, VIII, Letter XLII (*Fors Clavigera*).
28. *Works*, VI, 57 (*Sesame and Lilies*).
29. *Works*, VII, Letter V (*Fors Clavigera*).
30. *Works*, VI, 57 (*Sesame and Lilies*).
31. *Works*, VI, 177 (*Unto This Last*).

32. *Works*, XV, 34 (*The Crown of Wild Olive*).
33. *Works*, XIV, 130 (*Time and Tide*).
34. *Works*, XVIII, 268-69 (*Arrows of the Chase*).
35. *Works*, VII, Letter IV (*Fors Clavigera*).
36. *Works*, VII, Letter XVIII (*Fors Clavigera*).
37. *Works*, VII, Letter II (*Fors Clavigera*).
38. *Works*, VII, Letter IV (*Fors Clavigera*).
39. *Works*, VII, Letter VIII (*Fors Clavigera*).
40. *Works*, VI, 168-69 (*Unto This Last*).
41. *Works*, XIV, 177 (*Time and Tide*).
42. *Works*, XIV, 205 (*Time and Tide*).
43. *Works*, VII, Letter XI (*Fors Clavigera*).
44. *Works*, VII, Letter XI (*Fors Clavigera*).
45. *Works*, VIII, Letter XLIII (*Fors Clavigera*).
46. *Works*, XIV, 219 (*Time and Tide*).
47. *Works*, VIII, Letter XXXVI (*Fors Clavigera*).
48. William Gaunt, *The Aesthetic Adventure* (New York: Harcourt, Brace, 1945), p. 98.
49. *Works*, VIII, Letter XLVIII (*Fors Clavigera*).
50. *Works*, XIV, 234 (*Time and Tide*).
51. *Works*, IX, Letter LVII (*Fors Clavigera*).
52. Wilenski, *op. cit.*, p. 188.
53. Frederick Wilse Bateson, *English Poetry and the English Language: an Experiment in Literary History* (Oxford: Clarendon Press, 1934), p. 101.
54. *Works*, XV, 48 (*The Crown of Wild Olive*).
55. *Works*, VI, 159 (*Unto This Last*).
56. *Works*, VI, 163 (*Unto This Last*).
57. *Works*, VI, 163 (*Unto This Last*).
58. *Letters to Norton*, I, 245.
59. *Works*, XV, 49 (*The Crown of Wild Olive*).
60. *Works*, XIV, 136-37 (*Time and Tide*).
61. *Works*, VII, Letter I (*Fors Clavigera*).
62. *Works*, IX, Letter LXXXV (*Fors Clavigera*).
63. *Works*, IX, Letter LXXXV (*Fors Clavigera*).
64. E. R. and J. Pennell, *The Life of James McNeill Whistler* (Philadelphia: J. B. Lippincott Co., 1919), p. 167.
65. Cook, *op. cit.*, II, 184.
66. *Letters to Norton*, II, 78.
67. Morley, *Life of Cobden*, I, 213.
68. Cook, *op. cit.*, II, 129. Letter to Dr. John Brown, August, 1862.

69. *Works*, VIII, Letter XXXVI (*Fors Clavigera*).
70. *Works*, XVIII, 220 (Letter to *The Scotsman*, August 6, 1859, *Arrows of the Chase*).
71. *Works*, XVIII, 225 (*Arrows of the Chase*).
72. *Works*, VIII, Letter XLVIII (*Fors Clavigera*).
73. Leslie Stephen, "Mr. Ruskin's Recent Writings," *Fraser's Magazine*, June, 1874.

Five

JAMES THOMSON

1. Imogene B. Walker, *James Thomson (B.V.): A Critical Study* (Ithaca, N. Y.: Cornell University Press, 1950), p. 28.
2. *Ibid.*, p. 30.
3. H. S. Salt, *The Life of James Thomson (B. V.)* (London: Reeves and Turner, 1899), p. 52.
4. *Ibid.*, p. 16.
5. James Thomson, *Poetical Works*, ed. Bertram Dobell (London: Reeves and Turner, 1895), I, xxx-xxxi.
6. Paul Elmer More, *Shelburne Essays: Fifth Series* (New York: G. P. Putnam's Sons, 1917), pp. 170-95.
7. Walker, *op. cit.*, p. 28.
8. James Edward Meeker, *The Life and Poetry of James Thomson (B. V.)* (New Haven: Yale University Press, 1917), p. 85.
9. Dobell (ed.), *op. cit.*, p. 60.
10. Bertrand Russell, "A Free Man's Worship," *Mysticism and Logic, and other Essays* (New York: Longmans, Green, 1919), pp. 47-48.
11. Austin Warren, *Rage for Order: Essays in Criticism* (Chicago: University of Chicago Press, 1948), p. 66.
12. G. D. H. Cole, *Samuel Butler and The Way of All Flesh* (London: Home and Van Thal, 1947), p. 11.
13. Fyodor Dostoyevsky, *The Brothers Karamazov* (New York: Modern Library, 1929), pp. 78-79.
14. Herbert J. C. Grierson and J. C. Smith, *A Critical History of English Poetry* (New York: Oxford University Press, 1946), p. 440.
15. Knickerbocker, *Free Minds*, p. 100.
16. Russell, *Freedom versus Organization*, p. 131.

NOTES—CHAPTER FIVE—THOMSON

17. Cole and Postgate, *The British Common People: 1746-1938*, p. 199.
18. Thrall, *Rebellious Fraser's*, p. 148.
19. Cole and Postgate, *op. cit.*, p. 291.
20. Knickerbocker, *op. cit.*, p. 100.
21. William Rathbone Greg, *Rocks Ahead, or the Warnings of Cassandra* (Boston: J. R. Osgood and Co., 1875), p. 3.
22. Maccoby, *English Radicalism: 1853-1886*, p. 141.
23. Woodworth, *Christian Socialism in England*, p. 23.
24. *Ibid.*, p. 39.
25. Cole and Postgate, *op. cit.*, p. 291.
26. Woodworth, *op. cit.*, pp. 100-113.
27. Russell, *Freedom versus Organization*, p. 130.
28. *Ibid.*, p. 130.
29. Hugh Kingsmill, *The Progress of a Biographer* (London: Methuen, 1949), p. 23.
30. Ernest Belfort Bax, *Reminiscences and Reflection of a Mid and Late Victorian* (New York: T. Seltzer, 1920), pp. 17-18.
31. Hovell, *The Chartist Movement*, p. 57.
32. Glasier, *William Morris*, p. 164.
33. Knickerbocker, *op. cit.*, pp. 105-6.
34. Henry Mayers Hyndman, *Further Reminiscences* (London: Macmillan and Company, 1912), p. 140.
35. Walker, *op. cit.*, p. 44.
36. Maccoby, *op. cit.*, p. 143.
37. Cole and Postgate, *op. cit.*, p. 330.
38. *Ibid.*, p. 348.
39. George Bernard Shaw, *Sixteen Self Sketches* (New York: Dodd, Mead, 1949), pp. 93-94.
40. Maccoby, *op. cit.*, p. 143.
41. Hyndman, *Further Reminiscences*, pp. 140-41.
42. Salt, *op. cit.*, p. 304.
43. *Ibid.*, p. 304.
44. *Ibid.*, pp. 53-54.
45. Meeker, *op. cit.*, p. 61.
46. Salt, *op. cit.*, p. 301.
47. *Ibid.*, p. 301.
48. *Ibid.*, pp. 144-45.
49. *Ibid.*, p. 112.
50. Meeker, *op. cit.*, pp. 103-4.
51. Salt, *op. cit.*, p. 127.

52. Meeker, *op. cit.*, p. 71.
53. Meeker, *op. cit.*, p. 71; Salt, *op. cit.*, p. 302.
54. Meeker, *op. cit.*, pp. 71-72.
55. James Thomson, *Essays and Phantasies* (London: Reeves and Turner, 1887), p. 52.
56. Meeker, *op. cit.*, p. 100.
57. Salt, *op. cit.*, p. 301.

Six

DANTE GABRIEL ROSSETTI

1. William Michael Rossetti (ed.), *Dante Gabriel Rossetti: His Family Letters, with a Memoir* (Boston: Roberts, 1895), II, 63-69.
2. *Ibid.*, II, 42.
3. Oswald Doughty, *Dante Gabriel Rossetti, a Victorian Romantic* (London: F. Muller, 1949), p. 237.
4. William Michael Rossetti (ed.), *op. cit.*, II, 42.
5. Doughty, *op. cit.*, p. 237.
6. Gaunt, *The Pre-Raphaelite Tragedy*, p. 91.
7. Cook, *Life of Ruskin*, I, 501.
8. Doughty, *op. cit.*, p. 424.
9. John William Mackail, *The Life of William Morris* (New York: Longmans, Green, 1911), I, 109.
10. Georgiana Burne-Jones, *Memorials of Edward Burne-Jones* (New York: Macmillan Co., 1904), I, 164.
11. *Ibid.*, I, 149, 167.
12. Gaunt, *op. cit.*, p. 69.
13. British Broadcasting Corporation, *Ideas and Beliefs of the Victorians: an Historic Revaluation of the Victorian Age* (London: Sylvan Press, 1949), p. 372.
14. Norman Douglas, *South Wind* (New York: Modern Library, 1925), p. 104.
15. Shaw, *Works*, XIV, 61 (Preface to *Androcles and the Lion*).
16. Pearson, *The Smith of Smiths*, p. 238.
17. *Ibid.*, p. 71.
18. Sadleir, *Trollope: a Commentary*, p. 35.
19. Kingsmill, *Progress of a Biographer*, p. 5.
20. *Ibid.*, p. 10.
21. Shaw, *Works*, XIV, 147 (Preface to *Androcles and the Lion*).
22. Sadleir, *op. cit.*, p. 35.

NOTES—CHAPTER SIX—ROSSETTI 195

23. Morris, *News from Nowhere*, p. 64.
24. Bax, *Reminiscences*, p. 61.
25. Morris, *op. cit.*, p. 131.
26. Froude, *Thomas Carlyle: Life in London*, II, 18.
27. Joseph Freeman, *An American Testament; a Narrative of Rebels and Romantics* (New York: Farrar and Rinehart, 1936), p. 181.
28. Douglas, *op. cit.*, pp. 104-5.
29. Morris, *op. cit.*, p. 105.
30. Morley, *Life of Cobden*, I, 141.
31. Glasier, *William Morris*, p. 101.
32. Hyndman, *Further Reminiscences*, p. 102.
33. Hesketh Pearson, *G. B. S.: A Full-Length Portrait* (New York: Harper & Brothers, 1942), p. 366.
34. Florence Emily Hardy, *The Early Life of Thomas Hardy, 1840-1891* (New York: Macmillan Co., 1928), p. 315.
35. Florence Becker Lennon, *Victoria through the Looking-Glass; the Life of Lewis Carroll* (New York: Simon and Schuster, 1945), p. 132.
36. *Ibid.*, p. 7.
37. *Ibid.*, p. 4.
38. *Ibid.*, p. 323.
39. *Ideas and Beliefs of the Victorians*, p. 363.
40. George Bernard Shaw, *Man and Superman* (New York: Brentano's, 1905), p. 239.
41. Burne-Jones, *op. cit.*, I, 150.
42. Lord David Cecil, "Gabriel Charles Dante Rossetti," in *The Great Victorians*, ed. Harold John Massingham and Hugh Massingham (London: I. Nicholson and Watson, 1932), p. 440.
43. Louis Harap, *Social Roots of the Arts* (New York, International Publishers, 1949), p. 107.
44. Théophile Gautier, *Mademoiselle de Maupin* (New York: Modern Library, n. d.), pp. xxii-xxiii.
45. Edmond Adolphe Lepelletier, *Paul Verlaine, His Life—His Work* (New York: Duffield and Co., 1909), pp. 122-23.
46. *Ibid.*, pp. 165-66.
47. Quoted by Evelyn Waugh, *Rossetti, His Life and Work*, p. 216.
48. Doughty, *op. cit.*, p. 429.
49. *Ibid.*, p. 232.
50. *Ibid.*, p. 429.
51. *Ibid.*, p. 233.

52. Mackail, op. cit., II, 93-94.
53. Ibid., II, 94.
54. William Michael Rossetti (ed.), *Ruskin: Rossetti: Preraphaelitism: Papers 1854 to 1862* (London: George Allen, 1899), p. 306.
55. Doughty, op. cit., p. 157.
56. Waugh, op. cit., p. 98.
57. Doughty, op. cit., p. 330.
58. E. R. and J. Pennell, *The Life of James McNeill Whistler*, p. 132.
59. Gustaaf Johannes Renier, *Oscar Wilde* (London: P. Davies, 1933), p. 27.
60. Samuel C. Chew in Albert C. Baugh (ed.), *A Literary History of England* (New York: Appleton-Century-Crofts, 1948), p. 1424.
61. R. D. Waller, "The Blessed Damozel," *Modern Language Review*, XXVI (1931), 129.
62. Doughty, op. cit., p. 149.
63. Ibid., p. 199.
64. Frank Laurence Lucas, *Ten Victorian Poets* (Cambridge, Eng.: The University Press, 1948), p. 109.
65. Waugh, op. cit., p. 161.
66. Ibid., p. 14.
67. Ibid., p. 227.
68. Doughty, op. cit., p. 532.
69. Ibid., p. 149.
70. Ibid., p. 153.
71. Ibid., p. 130.
72. Ibid., p. 199.
73. Ibid., p. 226.
74. Waugh, op. cit., p. 107.
75. Gaunt, op. cit., p. 113.
76. Doughty, op. cit., p. 149.
77. Helen Rossetti Angeli, *Dante Gabriel Rossetti* (London: Hamilton, 1949), p. 195.
78. Waugh, op. cit., p. 110.
79. Doughty, op. cit., p. 301.
80. Ibid., p. 237.
81. Ibid., p. 371.
82. Ibid., p. 375.
83. Ibid., p. 278 and *passim*.
84. Waugh, op. cit., p. 107.

85. Doughty, *op. cit.*, p. 253.
86. *Ibid.*, p. 253.
87. *Ruskin-Rossetti Papers*, p. 40.
88. Waugh, *op. cit.*, p. 126.
89. Doughty, *op. cit.*, pp. 256-57.
90. *Ibid.*, pp. 292, 407.
91. *Ibid.*, p. 449.
92. Waugh, *op. cit.*, p. 175.
93. *Ibid.*, p. 175.
94. Gaunt, *op. cit.*, p. 131.
95. Frances Wickes, *The Inner World of Man* (New York: Farrar and Rinehart, 1938), p. 96.
96. William Michael Rossetti (ed.), *Ruskin: Rossetti: Preraphaelitism*, p. 89.
97. William Michael Rossetti (ed.), *Dante Gabriel Rossetti; his Family Letters*, I, 183.
98. Waugh, *op. cit.*, p. 147.
99. Walter Pater, *Appreciations, with an Essay on Style* (London: Macmillan and Co., 1922), p. 218.
100. Janet Camp Troxell, *Three Rossettis; Unpublished Letters to and from Dante Gabriel, Christina, William* (Cambridge: Harvard University Press, 1937), p. 49.
101. R. D. Waller, *op. cit.*, p. 140.
102. Stopford Brooke, *A Study of Clough, Arnold, Rossetti and Morris* (London: Pitman, 1908), p. 148.
103. Elton, *A Survey of English Literature, 1780-1880*, IV, 19.
104. Christopher Caudwell, *Illusion and Reality; A Study of the Sources of Poetry* (London: Macmillan, 1937), p. 55.

Seven

OSCAR WILDE

1. Samuel C. Chew in Albert C. Baugh (ed.), *A Literary History of England*, p. 1480.
2. George Moore, *Hail and Farewell* (New York: Appleton, 1914), I, 52.
3. George Bernard Shaw, *Plays: Pleasant and Unpleasant* (New York: Brentano's, 1905), p. viii.
4. Pearson, *G. B. S.*, p. 235.
5. Gustaaf Johannes Renier, *Oscar Wilde*, pp. 47-48.

6. Pearson, *op. cit.,* p. 195.
7. Henry Mayers Hyndman, *The Record of an Adventurous Life* (New York: Macmillan, 1911), p. 380; see also Hyndman, *Further Reminiscences,* p. 221.
8. Frances Winwar, *Oscar Wilde and the Yellow 'Nineties* (New York: Harper, 1940), p. 154.
9. *The Autobiography of William Butler Yeats* (New York: Macmillan, 1938), p. 119.
10. *The Picture of Dorian Gray* (New York: Modern Library, 1926), p. 65.
11. *Ibid.,* p. 19.
12. *Ibid.,* pp. 19-20.
13. Helen Merrell Lynd, *England in the Eighteen-Eighties: Toward a Social Basis for Freedom* (New York: Oxford University Press, 1945).
14. Maccoby, *English Radicalism: 1853-1886,* p. 237.
15. Hyndman, *Further Reminiscences,* p. 63.
16. Glasier, *William Morris,* p. 28.
17. Morris, *Signs of Change,* p. 6.
18. Gaunt, *The Pre-Raphaelite Tragedy,* p. 189.
19. Gaunt, *The Aesthetic Adventure,* p. 211.
20. Margaret Farrand Thorp, *Charles Kingsley* (Princeton, N. J.: Princeton University Press, 1937), pp. 118-19.
21. Hyndman, *Further Reminiscences,* p. 63.
22. *Ibid.,* p. 172.
23. Morley, *Life of Cobden,* I, 224.
24. Maccoby, *op. cit.,* p. 242.
25. Lloyd Wendell Eshleman, *A Victorian Rebel: The Life of William Morris* (New York: Scribner's, 1940), pp. 135-36.
26. Shaw, *Works,* XIV, 147 (*Androcles and the Lion*).
27. Gaunt, *The Aesthetic Aaventure,* p. 141.
28. *De Profundis* (New York: Modern Library, 1926), p. 318.
29. *The Complete Works of Oscar Wilde,* ed. Robert Ross (New York: Bigelow, Brown, 1921), IV, 28 (*The Decay of Lying*).
30. Tom Mann, *Tom Mann's Memoirs* (London: The Labour Publishing Co., 1923), p. 11.
31. Morris, *op. cit.,* pp. vii-viii.
32. Eshleman, *op. cit.,* p. 37.
33. *Ibid.,* p. 58.
34. Morris, *Signs of Change,* p. 2.
35. Morris, *News from Nowhere,* pp. 129-30.
36. Quoted by Oscar Maurer, Jr., in "William Morris and the

NOTES—CHAPTER SEVEN—WILDE

Poetry of Escape," *Nineteenth-Century Studies,* ed. Herbert Davis, William C. DeVane, and R. C. Bald (Ithaca, N. Y.: Cornell University Press, 1940), p. 273.
37. George Bernard Shaw, *William Morris As I Knew Him* (New York: Dodd, Mead, 1936), p. 46.
38. Shaw, *Collected Works,* XIV, 52-53 (*Androcles and the Lion*).
39. Shaw, *Plays: Pleasant and Unpleasant,* p. xxvi.
40. Hyndman, *Further Reminiscences,* p. 211.
41. Pearson, *G. B. S.,* p. 51.
42. L. W. Eshleman, *op. cit.,* p. 196.
43. Pearson, *op. cit.,* p. 51
44. Mann, *op. cit.,* p. 8.
45. Morris, *Signs of Change,* p. 103.
46. *Ibid.,* p. 18.
47. *Ibid.,* p. 32.
48. Gaunt, *The Pre-Raphaelite Tragedy,* p. 206.
49. Hyndman, *Further Reminiscences,* p. 118.
50. *Ibid.,* pp. 11-12.
51. *Ibid.,* p. 13.
52. *Ibid.,* p. 248.
53. *Ibid.,* p. 249.
54. *Ibid.,* p. 250.
55. *Ibid.,* p. 260.
56. *Ibid.,* p. 261.
57. *Ibid.,* p. 336.
58. *Ibid.,* p. 271.
59. *Ibid.,* p. 454.
60. *Works,* IV, 285 (*The Soul of Man under Socialism*).
61. *Works,* X, 265 (*The English Renaissance of Art*).
62. *Dorian Gray,* p. 19.
63. *Works,* IV, 285 (*The Soul of Man under Socialism*).
64. Abram Kardiner, *The Traumatic Neurosis of War* (New York, P. B. Hoeber, 1941).
65. *Works,* IV, 283 (*The Soul of Man under Socialism*).
66. *Works,* IV, 324 (*The Soul of Man under Socialism*).
67. *Works,* IV, 324 (*The Soul of Man under Socialism*).
68. Pearson, *op. cit.,* pp. 221-22.
69. Shaw, *Man and Superman,* p. xxxviii.
70. *Works,* IV, 326 (*The Soul of Man under Socialism*).
71. *Dorian Gray,* p. 86.
72. Norman Douglas, *South Wind,* p. 245.

73. Morris, *News from Nowhere*, p. 120.
74. *Dorian Gray*, p. 158.
75. *De Profundis*, p. 321.
76. Hesketh Pearson, *Oscar Wilde, His Life and Wit* (New York: Harper, 1946), p. 171.
77. *Works*, IV, 134 (*The Critic as Artist*).
78. *Dorian Gray*, p. 86.
79. *Works*, IV, 297 (*The Soul of Man under Socialism*).
80. *Dorian Gray*, p. 86.
81. *Autobiography of William Butler Yeats*, p. 115.
82. Renier, *Oscar Wilde*, p. 43.
83. *Works*, IV, 188 (*The Critic as Artist*).
84. Morris, *News from Nowhere*, p. 177.
85. Morris, *Signs of Change*, p. 122.
86. *Ibid.*, p. 140.
87. Glasier, *William Morris*, p. 145.
88. Morris, *News from Nowhere*, p. 228.
89. William Morris, *A Dream of John Ball* (London: Longmans, Green and Company, 1912), p. 33.
90. Gaunt, *The Pre-Raphaelite Tragedy*, p. 141.
91. *Works*, IV, 221 (*The Critic as Artist*).
92. *Dorian Gray*, p. 81.
93. *Ibid.*, p. 86.
94. *Works*, X, 176 (*Phrases and Philosophies for the Use of the Young*).
95. *Works*, IV, 135. (*The Critic as Artist*).
96. *De Profundis*, p. 292.
97. William York Tindall, *Forces in Modern British Literature* (New York: A. A. Knopf, 1947), p. 9.

INDEX

Althorp, Lord, 20
America, Arnold on, 53, 65, 66, 67, 68
Angeli, Helen Rossetti, 140
Aristocracy, 13, 17-18, 23, 38-39, 47-48, 50, 54, 65, 70, 82-83, 169; Carlyle on, 23, 38-39; Arnold on, 47-48, 50, 54, 65, 82-83, 169
Arnold, Matthew, 1, 3, 4, 8, 9, 40-85, 86, 87, 99, 104, 106, 107, 114, 115, 116, 126, 144, 150, 154, 158, 164, 168-69, 172-76, 178; personal integration, 40, 172-73; evidence of psychological conflict, 40-44; conflict reflected in poetry, 41-44, 76; feeling vs. intellect, 41-42; youth vs. age, 42; imaginative freedom vs. conformity, 42-43; spontaneity vs. moral effort, 43; unconscious vs. conscious, 43; interpretation of these conflicts, 44-45, 76; relationship to middle class, 45-56; philosophy of history, 45-56; empirical habit of mind, 46-47; flexibility, 47-49, 82; on dialectical advance in history, 49-52; on the *Zeitgeist*, 52; on the character of his age, 52-53; on the "perfected society," 54-56, 168-69; on aristocracy, 47-48, 50, 54, 65, 82-83, 169; on the state, 48, 50, 67, 84; on the middle class, 48-49, 65, 169; on the working class, 65, 169; on Hebraism and Hellenism, 50, 84; on the nation, 50-51; on the "powers" of the human spirit, 51, 55; on America, 53, 65, 66, 67, 68; ambivalent attitude toward the modern spirit, 7, 53-54, 64-73, 173-74; on "Jacobinism," 67, 68; on majorities, 68; on Ireland, 68; on the Zulu war, 68-69; his ambivalence a characteristic of the middle class, 70-71; further affinities with the middle class, 71; effect of ambivalent attitudes on poetry and criticism, 73-85; limitations as critic of society, 77-85; the theory of culture, 77-79, 83-85, 174, 175; the role of ideas, 78-79, 83-85, 174; the role of institutional change, 78, 82-85, 174; disparagement of action, 78-82; on disinterestedness, 79-82; on the French Revolution, 83-84; on the Puritan inheritance, 84; compared with Carlyle and Ruskin, 174-75
Ashburton, Lord, 38
Authoritarian character structure, in Carlyle, 29-35; in Ruskin, 97-98
Aveling, Edward, 116

Barker, Ernest, 72
Bateson, Frederick Wilse, 98
Baudelaire, Charles, 132, 133
Bax, E. Belfort, 7, 112, 129
Bellamy, Edward, 151
Bentham, Jeremy, 23, 47; *see also* Utilitarianism
Biblical criticism, 107
Bismarck, Otto Eduard Leopold von, 68
Bradlaugh, Charles, 106, 113, 114-15, 118, 119
Bragman, Louis, 89
Bright, John, 158
Brooke, Stopford, 145
Brougham, Henry Peter, 19, 22, 60
Brown, Edward Killoran, 81
Browning, Robert, 143
Buchanan, Robert, 134, 143
Burke, Edmund, 52
Burke, Kenneth, 41
Burne-Jones, Sir Edward, 123, 124, 125, 131, 155
Butler, Samuel, 32, 44, 106

Caine, Hall, 133
Calvinism, 15, 31
Carlyle, Jane Welsh, 24
Carlyle, Thomas, 1, 3, 4, 7, 8, 9, 13-39, 41, 50, 55, 56, 72, 73, 77, 86, 87, 92, 98, 99, 104, 105, 126, 129, 144, 150, 154, 164, 169, 170-73, 174-76, 178; religious views, 14-15; family relationships, 15; on the organic society, 15; on aristocracy, 23, 38-39; on middle class, 23-24, 39; on political economists, 23-24; psychological

conflicts in, 3, 26-29; authoritarian character structure, 29-35; distrust of democracy, 32-35; on the "hero," 34-35; advocacy of individual reform, 36, 37, 175; on Mammonism, 36; on education, 36-37; Rectorship Address, 37; reasons for popularity, 37-39; compared with Ruskin, 170-72
Carroll, Lewis, 143
Caudwell, Christopher, 146
Cecil, Lord David, 106, 107, 119
Chartism, 4, 5, 14, 21, 26, 35, 56, 57, 58, 59, 61, 62, 86, 111, 115, 121, 152, 159, 169, 170
Chew, Samuel, 148
Christian Socialism, 59, 110, 111
Clough, Arthur Hugh, 43, 107, 114
Cobbett, William, 18, 20, 59
Cobden, Richard, 61, 130, 158
Cole, G. D. H., 6, 16, 21, 57, 115, 126
Coleridge, Samuel Taylor, 146
Combination Acts, repeal of, 25
Comte, Auguste, 51, 54
Condorcet, Jean Antoine, 51
Corn Laws, agitation against, 5, 21, 54, 61, 62, 168
Cornforth, Fanny, 140, 142
Craven, F., 135
Crimean War, 62, 152
Criticism, psychological, 2-3, 8-10; social, 4, 6, 8-10
Culture, Arnold on, 77-79, 83-85, 174

Dante Alighieri, 134, 139
Darwin, Charles, 107, 151
Dickens, Charles, 19, 20
Disinterestedness, Arnold on, 79-82
Disraeli, Benjamin, 38, 57, 115
Dobell, Bertram, 106
Doughty, Oswald, 134, 139, 141
Douglas, Norman, 126, 162

Eastlake, Lady, 59
Eliot, George, 115, 117
Elton, Oliver, 146
Emerson, Ralph Waldo, 24, 32, 41, 145
Engels, Friedrich, 169
Estheticism, 8, 80, 131-36, 153, 177; in Rossetti, 132-36, 177
Evangelicalism, 58-59, 86, 109
Eyre, Edward John, Governor of Jamaica, 32

Factory conditions, 13, 15-17
Fitzgerald, Edward, 104, 106, 107
Foote, G. W., 117

Freeman, Joseph, 129
French Revolution, 22, 66, 70, 78, 83-84, 109; Arnold on, 83-84
Freud, Sigmund, 2, 10
Fromm, Erich, 10, 11, 29-31, 75
Froude, James Anthony, 28, 59
Fuller, Margaret, 34

Gaskell, Elizabeth, 57, 58
Gaunt, William, 97
Gautier, Théophile, 132, 133
George, Henry, 111, 151, 157
Goethe, Johann Wolfgang von, 41, 46
Grand Consolidated Trades Union, 25
Greg, William Rathbone, 7, 110
Guérin, Eugénie de, 41
Guérin, Maurice de, 41
Guild of St. Matthew, 111

Halévy, Elie, 6, 58, 61
Halliday, James L., 3, 28, 29
Hammond, Barbara, 7
Hammond, John Lawrence, 7
Hardy, Thomas, 11, 104, 106, 107, 130
Harrison, Frederic, 54
Headlam, Stewart, 111
Hebraism, 50, 84
Hegel, Georg Wilhelm Friedrich, 51
Heine, Heinrich, 158
Hellenism, 50, 84
Hetherington, Henry, 25, 113, 114, 116
Hemingway, Ernest, 9
Henley, William Ernest, 153, 163
Herder, Johann Gottfried, 51
Hill, G. B., 134
Horney, Karen, 10
Housman, Alfred Edward, 11, 104
Hovell, Mark, 6, 26
Howell, Charles Augustus, 124, 140
Humanitarianism, 58
Hunt, Holman, 87, 122, 123, 124
Huxley, Aldous, 75
Huxley, Thomas Henry, 72, 73, 115, 151
Hyndman, Henry Mayers, 7, 130, 151, 152, 157, 158, 159

Industrial conditions, 13, 15-17
Ingersoll, Robert Green, 151

Jacobinism, Arnold on, 67, 68
Jingoism, 152-53
Jones, Howard Mumford, 72
Joubert, Joseph, 41, 66

Kafka, Franz, 146
Kardiner, Abram, 160
Keats, John, 134

INDEX

Kingsley, Charles, 59, 110, 111, 152
Kingsmill, Hugh, 112, 128
Kipling, Rudyard, 68, 153
Knickerbocker, Frances Wentworth, 7, 114

La Touche, Rose, 88
Leopardi, Giacomo, 118
Leopold, Prince, 102
Linnell, Alfred, 158
London Working Men's Association, 25, 170
Lovett, William, 25
Lucas, Frank Lawrence, 137
Ludlow, J. M., 111
Lynd, Helen Merrell, 7, 151

Macaulay, Thomas Babington, 11, 52, 72, 73
Maccoby, Simon, 7, 57, 63
Mackail, John William, 125
Maginn, William, 19, 23, 38
Malory, Sir Thomas, 134, 155
Malthus, Thomas Robert, 19, 151
Mann, Tom, 7, 154, 157, 159
Marcus Aurelius, 41
Martineau, Harriet, 27
Marx, Karl, 110, 151, 157, 169
Maurice, Frederick Denison, 59, 111
Methodism, 59
Michelet, Jules, 51
Middle class, 14, 18-22, 23-24, 39, 45-46, 48-49, 65, 70, 154, 169; Carlyle on, 23-24, 39; Arnold's affinities with, 45-56; Arnold on, 48-49, 65, 169; Wilde on, 154
Mill, John Stuart, 17, 23, 31, 37, 97, 100, 103, 151
Millais, John Everett, 124
Mitchell, T. M., 89
Modern spirit, Arnold's ambivalent attitude toward, 7, 53-54, 64-73, 173-74
Moore, George, 148
More, Paul Elmer, 106, 107, 119
Morley, John, 61, 68, 69, 102, 109, 127
Morris, Jane Burden, 124, 139, 141
Morris, William, 11, 14, 22, 25, 32, 40, 44, 55, 67, 69-70, 71, 75, 106, 113, 114, 123, 124, 127, 129, 130, 135, 142, 148, 151, 152, 153, 154, 155, 156, 157, 159, 160, 161, 162, 164, 165, 178

Nelson, Louise, 89
Newman, John Henry, 72
Norton, Charles Eliot, 88, 102, 135

Oastler, Robert, 38

O'Brien, Bronterre, 62, 159
O'Connor, Feargus, 57, 62
Owen, Robert, 25, 110, 116, 152

Pater, Walter, 80, 133, 136, 145, 153
Pearson, Hesketh, 18
Peterloo Massacre, 18, 127
Place, Francis, 21
Plint, T. E., 135
Political economists, Carlyle on, 23-24; Ruskin on, 93-94
Poor Law, 17, 21; agitation against, 5, 21, 26, 38, 56, 169
Postgate, Raymond, 6
Pre-Raphaelite Brotherhood, 121, 123, 133
Princep, Val, 125
Prudery, Victorian, 130-31

Ranke, Leopold von, 51
Rectorship Address, by Carlyle, 37
Reform Bill, First (1832), 4, 5, 13, 18, 19, 21, 25, 54, 56, 86, 159, 168
Reform Bill, Second (1867), 57, 67, 115
Religious belief, *see* under Victorian society and under individual authors
Renier, Gustaaf Johannes, 149
Revolution of 1848, 65
Reynolds, Sir Joshua, 123
Rimbaud, Jean Nicolas Arthur, 132
Rossetti, Christina, 131
Rossetti, Dante Gabriel, 1, 4, 5, 7, 8, 9, 90, 121-47, 150, 153, 154, 155, 160, 165, 166, 173, 176-78; promise in youth, 121-26; his estheticism, 132-36, 177; supremacy of art, 133-34; amoralism, 134-35; detachment from political concerns, 135; contempt for man of business, 135-36; achievement in poetry and art, 136; failure to fulfill promise, 136-37; failure in personal integration, 137-47, 177; a consequence partly of the esthete's isolation, 138-47, 177; religious views, 142; interest in the occult, 143; obsessional interests, 143; paranoid symptoms, 143-45; esoteric character of his work, 146
Rossetti, William Michael, 135
Ruskin, John, 1, 3, 5, 7, 8, 9, 14, 32, 45, 55, 72, 73, 86-103, 104, 105, 124, 125, 126, 127, 144, 150, 154, 155, 158, 164, 169, 170-73, 174-76, 178; motives in turning from art to social criticism, 86-87; abandonment of religious belief, 87; psychological

conflicts in, 3, 87-91, 97; relationship with parents, 87-88; effect of neurosis on work, 89-92; sources of strength as social critic, 91-92; on poverty amid plenty, 92; new morality in conflict with Christianity, 92-93; attack on political economists, 93-94; analysis of personal relationships in an industrial society, 94-96; on interest, 94-95; on wealth, 95-96; inadequacy of constructive proposals, 96-97; outlook circumscribed by psychic authoritarianism, 97-98; on the criminal, 98; on liberty, 98; appeal to individual conscience, 98-102, 175; on war, 100; "inspirational" passages, 102; invectives, 102-3; compared with Carlyle, 170-72
Russell, Bertrand, 16, 17, 57, 61, 108, 109, 112

Sadleir, Michael, 128
Sadler, Michael, 38
Saintsbury, George, 71, 81
Salt, H. S., 106, 116, 118
Scott, William Bell, 142
Seccombe, Thomas, 58
Secularist movement, 5, 106, 113, 114-16, 118, 119, 121, 151, 176
Shaftesbury, Lord (Anthony Ashley Cooper, 1st Earl of Shaftesbury), 19, 20, 24, 38, 58
Shaw, George Bernard, 33, 115, 126, 131, 148, 149, 153, 154, 156, 157, 159, 161, 178
Shelley, Percy Bysshe, 113, 114, 115, 116, 117
Siddal, Elizabeth, 137, 139-42, 144
Smith, Sydney, 37, 38, 127
Society for the Diffusion of Useful Knowledge, 22, 60, 115
Society for the Promotion of Working Men's Associations, 111
Spencer, Herbert, 26-27, 151
State power, Arnold on, 48, 50, 67, 84
"Steam Intellect Society," see Society for the Diffusion of Useful Knowledge
Stephen, Leslie, 103
Stephens, James Rayner, 38
Stillman, W. J., 134
Swinburne, Algernon Charles, 11, 106, 114, 124, 133, 134, 140, 141

Tennyson, Alfred, 11, 16, 72, 73, 104, 107, 108, 112, 114, 134, 152
Thiers, Louis Adolphe, 95

Thomson, James, 1, 2, 3, 5, 7, 8, 9, 104-20, 121, 144, 145, 150, 151, 173, 176-78; pessimism attributable in part to psychic abnormality, 104-5, 177; in part to death of Matilda Weller, 105-6; in part to philosophic naturalism, 106-8; attitude toward religious belief not typically Victorian, 113-14; relationship to Secularist movement, 114-20; further explanation of his pessimism, 118-20, 176-77
Thrall, Miriam, 6
Tindall, William York, 167
Tractarianism, 109, 110
Trade-unionism, 25-26
Traill, H. D., 156
Transcendentalism, 15, 22
Trilling, Lionel, 72
Tyndall, John, 115

Utilitarianism, 14, 18, 19

Verlaine, Paul, 132, 133
Victorian society, insecurity in, 6, 7, 17-18, 56-64; need for "structuralized" understanding of, 11; industrial conditions, 13, 15-17; child labor, 15-16; aristocracy, 13, 17-18, 70; middle class, 14, 18-22, 70; working class, 14, 20-22, 25-26, 70-71; working class support of middle-class policies, 61-63; trade unionism, 25-26; humanitarianism, 58; Evangelicalism, 58-59, 86, 109; role of mass pressures, 63-64; ideas regarded as principal agent of historical change, 82; remedy for evil sought in appeal to individual conscience, 98-99; religious belief, 7-8, 12, 14, 176; religious revival, 58-60, 109; undermining of foundations of traditional belief, 106-8; psychological function of religious belief, 108-9, 175-76; social function, 109-13; ethical values in an acquisitive society, 126, 170; respectability, propriety, and moral strictness, 126-30; prudery, 130-31; ideological ferment of 1880's and 1890's, 151-54; threat of war in 1880's and 1890's, 152-53; jingoism, 152-53

Walker, Imogene B., 105
Walker, R. D., 137
Waugh, Evelyn, 138, 140
Weller, Matilda, 106
Wesley, John, 59

/ N D E X

Westbury, Lord, 110
Whistler, James Abbott McNeill, 97, 101, 133, 136
Wickes, Frances, 143
Wilde, Oscar, 1, 4, 5, 7, 8, 9, 133, 134, 135, 136, 148-67, 173, 176, 178, 179; representative of a new time spirit, 148-49; leader of a "revolution in morals," 149; morbid trends, 149-50; confidence in spontaneous side of his nature, 150; psychological insights, 150-51; attitude toward middle class, 154; stress on social structure rather than on individual, 154; shares outlook of Morris and Shaw, 159; and of Rossetti, 160; new ethical outlook, 161-67, 179; rejection of immutable human nature, 161-62; reversal of ethical norms, 163-64; conception of self-realization compared with that of Morris, 164-65; advocacy of ethical neutrality, 165-66; stress on unification of the personality, 166-67
Wilenski, R. H., 3, 88, 98
Williams-Ellis, Amabel, 3, 88
Wilson, Dover, 72
Wolfe, Thomas, 8-9
Woolf, Leonard, 72
Wordsworth, William, 41, 126
Working class, 14, 20-22, 25-26, 61-63, 65, 70-71, 169; support of middle-class policies, 61-63; Arnold on, 65, 169
Working Men's College, 125

Yeats, William Butler, 135, 150
Young, George Malcolm, 16